BE AND IT WILL BE

Surrender your Ego and Move into God

By Ronny Hatchwell and Zach Sivan

Copyright © 2005 by Ronny Hatchwell and Zach Sivan

Copyright Year: 2005

Copyright Notice: by Ronny Hatchwell and Zach Sivan. All rights reserved.

ISBN 978-1-4092-0222-6

http://www.beanditwillbe.com

Be and it will Be

Table of Contents

Introduction	6
Chapter one – who is sol	13
Chapter two – free choice – no "right" or "wrong"	20
Chapter three – state of being	31
Chapter four – practicing the state of being	41
Chapter five – thoughts and meditation	52
Chapter six – practicing meditation	62
Chapter seven – the ego	69
Chapter eight – desire and to let go	73
Chapter nine – letting go of the ego	86
Chapter ten – taking responsibility	95
Chapter eleven – serenity	105
Chapter twelve – thought management	117
Chapter thirteen – managing your feelings	128
Chapter fourteen – getting messages from the universe	136
Chapter fifteen – the secret of wavelengths	146
Chapter sixteen – discover who you are	153
Chapter seventeen - surrendering to the God within you	163
Epilogue	174
About the authors	177

Be and it will Be

INTRODUCTION

It is an ordinary Saturday afternoon and Ronny and I are playing with the idea of writing a book with SOL. We are both very excited about the idea of working with her on this book to share our journey and her teachings.

We first want to see what SOL has to say about writing a book. Ronny is getting into her special meditation and "calls" on SOL to communicate with us. SOL is not channeled through speech, but through writing. As the messages are received, Ronny types them up simultaneously. It looks very natural for an onlooker – a woman typing on her computer. I guess that this looks so natural to a rational person like myself, that I can accept this form of communication with SOL.

The idea is to write a book about our experiences of enlightenment through our sessions together. We believe that a book like this would help to remind people that they already have the ability to be enlightened, and that these sessions will help them recover this "recalled memory."

SOL suggested that we start by explaining how she first entered our dimension and in particular, how Ronny became the vessel through which to be channeled. Ronny reads her little prayer which is a request to be a positive channeller on behalf of SOL.

The Dialogue begins:

>Ronny: SOL, are you here?

>SOL: Yes my child.

>Zach: SOL, we would like to write a book with you and do not know how and where to start. Please could you advise us?

>SOL: At last! You have made the right decision. This will be a very rewarding experience but it might take some time. Are you happy to go ahead?

>Ronny: Yes. Perhaps you could tell us something about what the name SOL signifies.

SOL: Sometime in the eighteenth-century there were two brothers who left Spain. One of them went to England while the other, a chief rabbi, traveled to Fez in Morocco. There he had a beautiful daughter named Solika. The Sultan's son of Morocco wanted to marry Solika but being of Jewish faith, she refused and as a punishment, she was stoned, beheaded and dragged through the town. The Sultan, just before his death, felt such remorse for what he had done that he ordered a monument to be built in her honor. To this day both Muslims and Jews visit the grave to receive blessings. SOL is short for Solika Hatchuel.

Zach: Thank you SOL. Perhaps you could give us a short explanation on how you entered our dimension through Ronny.

Ronny: Perhaps Zach, if you understand how this happened, the rest will fall into place

Over the years I have had out of body and telepathic, experiences. The first time it happened was when I was a child. I was playing in my parent's friends' pool in their back yard when I found myself drowning. I could see my friends sitting by the side of the pool above me, calling to my father. My father jumped into the pool, grabbed me and lay me on the grass and

Be and it will Be

tried to pump out the water from my lungs. Even though I was unconscious I could clearly see every thing that was going on around me. My perspective was from above. And although I believe this may not be such an unusual experience, there have been many instances since when I have had out of body experiences and also have been able to foresee things in the future.

I kept hearing stories about this spiritual being, SOLIKA. Throughout my childhood I had remembered my father mentioning her as a family legend, and although my family's name is spelled Hatchwell and hers Hatchuel, I was told that we derived from the same family tree. Stories like this made me feel very close to Solika.

At a certain time in my life I was in crisis, my marriage had collapsed, I was a single mother, I was living on the breadline and I was at the point of an emotional breakdown when I heard a voice in my head saying that I should take a pen and paper and write. I felt a tremendous pressure down the back of the left side of my head. There was suddenly a rush through my right arm, and I started to write! I was absolutely amazed when I found that I had written that I would see a male friend I had not seen in five years and that I would earn twenty-four and a half shekels that day… which was not too inspiring! It was signed "your spiritual guide, SOL."

I crunched up the note, put it in my pocket and forgot all about it. By the end of that day I had met one of my brother's friends from England whom I had not seen in five years and found that I had earned exactly twenty-four and a half shekels selling the wooden toys that I made for a living at that time. And then it all hit me!

During the following few weeks, I found myself going through the same procedure – voice, pen, paper, forecast – until one day SOL began to explain that she was an intelligence, who at some point had been Solika. And in this capacity of "being" and "Intelligence" SOL had been able to attach herself to other intelligences, and thus manifest what we call "Acts of God."

As a Medium and a Channeller, SOL is able to allow me to receive information which would be interesting to us as human beings. I have lived actively with SOL for eighteen years and I believe that I am SOL and She is my Higher Power, my connection to the All That Is, which is part of all of us. We each channel but most of us are unaware of this capacity. All it takes is awareness. If one God, one Energy, one Intelligence created All That Is, and created us in his/her image, then He/She created lots of smaller gods, all creating

His/Her subjective worlds. Therefore you and I are one and the same.

Be and it will Be

Zach: Perhaps at this point we should also include in the book how I came to know Ronny and how my life has changed as she channeled SOL for me.

Around two years ago, a friend of mine, Nurit, told me about Ronny and her ability to channel what she called "valuable information from a higher intelligence". I must admit that I was very skeptical. In fact, I was at that time, and in a way still am, very skeptical about any mystical forms of guidance such as horoscope reading, numerology, etc., and considered Ronny's channeling to be in the same category. Nonetheless, I felt that Nurit had good judgment and I was at a point in my life when I needed help with my relationships with women. I was twenty-seven years old and hadn't yet maintained a steady, healthy relationship. My previous relationships with women had been purely physical rather than emotional. I also had a relative at that time who was forty-five years old and still dating endlessly and I thought it may have had something to do with our family genes! It seemed so chauvinistic and yet I never saw myself as a chauvinist.

So I had asked Nurit if she could help me find a soul mate and help me build a healthy lasting relationship. Nurit offered to take a note with a few questions to Ronny. I did not know Ronny at that time and I was very surprised when Nurit told me that Ronny didn't have to know anything about me except my name. This made me even more suspicious but also somewhat curious.

A few days later Nurit came back with the answer from Ronny. It was overwhelming! It was as if the answer came from somebody who knew me better than I knew myself. SOL, you spoke of my family background and how all of this led to my inability to attach myself emotionally to any special companion. You identified a fundamental pattern in my relationship with my mother that was actually the source of my behavior with other women. I wasn't even aware of that pattern at the time and my first reaction was, how does she know all this about me?

Once I had overcome my amazement, I sat down and read your answer more carefully and realized that this came from a place, an intelligence, I had never encountered before. It was very clear-cut and profound and most of all, painfully accurate. SOL continued by addressing things that I was constantly evading. I found out for example that I had a great fear of rejection, and this was very surprising, as I had always thought of myself as being quite invulnerable. And so I embarked on this journey with you, Ronny and SOL and here we are, writing our book

CHAPTER ONE

Who is SOL

On my first visit to Ronny I found myself surprised and relieved to find that Ronny was an ordinary person who had a regular day job in the local music industry. As our conversations grew, this opened a whole new and substantial chapter in my life.

It started with long conversations with Ronny trying to work out the mystery of SOL's presence and then led me into a journey of self-discovery with regards to my relationship problems. During this journey SOL guided me through various awareness levels and the different obstacles I had to solve on my way to a new "Self." This was a major journey for me. And I am happy to say that this journey has led me to find and marry my soul mate and start a family for the first time. I have a close and intimate relationship with my wife and two children whom I adore. In terms of my career, I have gone from having a regular job to becoming a partner in my own company. These have been huge steps forward as I overcame my fears with SOL's help.

What I absolutely love about your philosophy, SOL, is that your channeled information is also so very practical. I have learnt that to get what we wish for we have to make changes. That is why I am so excited to embark on this journey of change and to set it down in this book.

Firstly SOL, I would like to ask you who you are.

SOL: I am who, what and everything I wish to be. I am the purest of energies on whatever level I choose to be at any moment in time, to manifest physically or to stay as pure information. I am not a spirit but a high-level energy, which is closer to All That Is energy. I work on wavelengths - the wavelengths of intelligence or information, as you would call it. I can and I do at times attach myself to other energies when certain matters need to be influenced. When Ronny channels me I am a part of her intelligence. It is like water flowing into a glass or a jug. The quality of water does not change, only the quantity. So all intelligence is one and the same but when it is split into two different mediums the

Be and it will Be

Intelligence still keeps the same quality in both. This One intelligence is always One.

As you go further with your questions I shall touch on this subject again so it will be clearer to you.

Zach: Let me see if I can understand this. Although we have a number of things in common you do not seem to be of the same world as I. Why are you and I different?

SOL: We are not different except that I have the knowledge to be where I want to be at this time as a result of a certain level of awareness which I have attained in my previous life, and which I am *now* and you are not *now*. You see Zach, there is no other world. All worlds are here and now. Since you are in a body and are manifested as Zach, and you have not yet reached spiritual awareness, you are unable to access these worlds as yet. This does not mean that when you leave your body this time around you will be able to access all worlds, as it will depend on your level of awareness at that time. Your energy will decide for you how it wishes to go on and what the choices are whenever this happens.

Zach: I must say that I feel a little envious of you as you can be and do whatever you like whenever you like and I am quite limited in comparison.

SOL: Absolutely - I agree - I would not trade places with you for anything! However, I have had my share at your level of awareness. In fact I had been through many manifestations and I simply completed them. One of them was as Solika of Fez.

Zach, there isn't a better or worse choice of awareness. Your choice, or if you prefer it, the choice of All That Is, is when every single soul has decided and chosen that you should be Zach, at this particular time. Because you must remember that you are part of a huge picture and you play a vital role for the greater understanding. Just as mine and Ronny's roles are. Think of it as a Shakespearean play where the different actors each hold an important part without which the play could not be staged. Every single player is vital to the whole. I'm sorry that you are not happy with your part but I shall let you into a secret. Within your given situation you can choose to change your part.

Zach: You have already told me that there is no good or bad, right or wrong, better or worse, but I know that sometimes I like certain things and sometimes I do not like others.

Be and it will Be

SOL: Zach, you see things that way because you are limited. Oh, I do not mean to offend you, but you operate on a certain level of understanding and you filter what you hear through certain levels of awareness.

I will explain. I say that there is only CREATION + FREE CHOICE which results in KNOWLEDGE. Everything else is a matter of what you decide to add to this equation. This will probably be because of your conditioning and the way you were brought up and how you chose to react and feel toward your peers. Today you are an adult and no one can tell you how to feel, you make these choices yourself at every level.

I always say try to enjoy everything that you do and don't do something if you feel you will not enjoy it. Yes, even if it is something that you feel may be *bad*, you can in fact turn it around by changing your attitude towards whatever it is. I am not saying that you have to feel good at all times. For example, the sadness you feel when a close person dies. What I am saying is that you should enjoy or accept the feeling. In this case I suggest detachment and allowing yourself to see matters from a different level of awareness so that you can see the full picture. I promise you that when you next come across a similar situation and you allow yourself to fully feel the experience, it will be much easier.

Zach: I would like you to expand on this issue about feelings later on in the book. At this point I would like to understand better the question of who we are and what we are doing here. According to your previous answers it seems that it is all a matter of different levels of awareness, so where does it begin and where does it end?

SOL: Zach, why do you need to know?

Zach: I think it is important to find meaning in what I do and who I am and I think that people who read this book would also like to know.

SOL: Commendable! You have the better good of all at heart, Zach!

Everything began with One energy, the same energy that has and still exists through time and dimension. This One energy just happened at one point in time to divide itself so that it could discover for itself who and what it is in every possible aspect.

Be and it will Be

There will come a time when you will have a flash of awareness of all infinite probabilities and *know* yourself through this energy. That is when you will become one with the One which you are part of.

This is a very difficult concept at your level of being. As I said previously, you are limited because of the choices you made and those which were made for you in this physical dimension. I say you made, as you are part of the One.

I am going to disappoint you because there is no meaning. Looking for a meaning is your way of justifying your existence. *You are here.* Once you accept this you will be a lot happier. *It simply is* because the One has chosen it to be. That is all.

CHAPTER TWO

Free Choice – no "right" or "wrong"

One Month Later

    Zach: Hi SOL. I'm trying to overcome one of the most terrible experiences I have ever had in my life and I don't know how to handle it.

    My uncle who was my very dear friend, Ethan committed suicide two weeks ago. This was a terrible shock and a great loss for me, and the fact that it was a suicide, makes it doubly difficult. I guess I feel guilty, almost as if I could have prevented it myself, but I know on a rational level that I could not, or maybe that is my way of convincing myself that there was no way of stopping him, so I can ease these feelings of guilt. Ethan was so gifted, so smart, so full of potential, that I can't help wondering how someone so talented could end up committing suicide. He was a joy to everyone around him as he brought music to their lives as a professional DJ. He created wonderful evenings for friends, selecting from his rare collection of records, wonderful music for our enjoyment. It was as if he was telling beautiful stories through his music. I would spend hours listening as he played, losing all sense of time.

However, Ethan was mentally ill. I guess this is the first time that I have been able to admit that Ethan was seriously ill. I have tried to deny this fact for such a long time. Ethan was a drug addict and he had become very depressed because of his excessive use of drugs. He never really told me what and how much he took, but I also believe I chose to turn a blind eye and denied Ethan's drug use. He spent the last weeks of his life at his mother's complaining repeatedly about his miserable life and blaming God and everyone around him for his situation. At one point it just became impossible to listen to his repeated complaints and this is probably one of the reasons I feel guilty. In our last conversation I refused to address his issues and I just got annoyed at his endless grumbling. I feel so bad about it now.

After our last conversation, SOL, I was very confused when you said there is no meaning as to why we are here. And now, after this terrible tragedy I'm even more confused!

SOL: Zach, do not confuse feelings with the search for why you are here. Why are you always searching for the meaning for why you were born - I say that there is no meaning to why you were born - you just *were*, since that is what the All That Is wanted. This does not, however, take away from the fact that it is up to you to make your life meaningful, you have already spent too much time searching for the "wrong" answer. You are here and that is it. There is no meaning in that. It simply is. You must make what you choose to go through in your life meaningful and this is done by experiencing your life to the fullest. Once you make your life meaningful you will come to know the meaning of life.

Zach: Let me see if I understand. The answer to the question "why are we here" is "You just are here." Once we accept that our being here is just to be here, we have to find meaning in what we are doing here. Is that correct?

SOL: You do not have to search for the meaning - the meaning will come to you through *being*. It is a discovery of what is already here, not something you have to invent. God has it all already created. It is already in the unconscious, in the dimension of thought. You, as an aspect of God, have the opportunity to discover these "thoughts" and manifest them into the physical dimension on behalf of All That Is. This is your call - you are part of All That Is - you are not separate or on another level of awareness. You *will* know All That Is as yourself and therefore *know* that there is no meaning except that you just are.

Zach: So what you are saying is that every thing *just is* as you say and there is no right or wrong. So why is it that a person committing suicide affects so many people around him so strongly - and I'm not just talking about the issue of death but also about the issue of someone taking their own life. Why can't we say, "well, it is just how it is," and just go on?

SOL: Zach you can say anything you like. You are confusing two separate issues. Your question was to do with why you are here. To this I say because you are! Accept that and be done with it, so that you can move on to what really is important and that is... that you are here!

As you are here you have an opportunity to create - creation is on every level even on the level you call right or wrong. Every thing you do is creation simply because it is manifested from thought, from ideas, from the unwritten.

You see, there is another world from the current world you operate in, think of it as a *see-through world* - you cannot see it, take it from me it does exist. You can take this dimension and manifest it into the physical world through your choices. Someone taking their own life is a choice from all the possibilities in the *see-through* world. This is what Ethan chose to experience for himself and for those around him which includes you. Everything we choose is so that we can know ourselves better. Every experience brings out a reaction and thus we have a mirror to our internal subjective world.

Oh yes, I grant you that this would not be an experience I myself would choose, although in my past life as Solika, one of the choices I made was to be killed for not fulfilling someone's wishes. And that was my finale.

Zach, in the physical form, you were given senses and feelings. These are your guides and you must use them correctly. You cannot deny what you feel as this would be denying who you are. You must confront your feelings in order to discover how important or how unimportant, they are.

Zach: I'm sorry if I'm going in circles here, SOL, but Ethan was very depressed. He felt that there is no hope. If we take into consideration that there is no meaning for us to be here then why not end this "being here" in situations like this?

SOL: Don't be sorry, Zach. You wish to understand and we will continue discussing this until you do. Please understand this though. There is no end, it is a cycle, a circle rather than a straight line. A circle simply goes on - in fact everything in the All That Is is a circle. Even if Ethan took his own life in this physical form, he still continues. He cannot end simply as he, and everyone else, is part of God - God is the beginning and the end and simply is. You must accept the fact that creation simply happened because God chose it. The fact is that you are part of this creation and therefore you can be an aspect of God, discovering for God, the reason you are here. You are obliged as part of mankind to find the way to a higher level of awareness for and on behalf of God. I shall let you into a secret - there is a short cut to getting to this higher level and it is through making the choice of positive thinking.

Zach: It still doesn't explain why we should not take our own life when we are troubled and depressed. As you may know I was raised in a very religious environment and therefore committing suicide was considered a sin.

SOL: All religions speak in the name of God. Religions are man-made - they usually emerge when a group of people has come through an incomprehensible experience which has brought them fear. Over the generations, these religions have separated the human race from the TRUTH, which is that God, their creator, was within them all the time. God is not separate. And religion in fact has become a God - you might even say another God. All the rules and regulations have taken over and the essence of "love thy neighbor as you would your self", has gotten lost on the way. The Catholic religion for example knew of the *unwritten law*, which the Jewish people know as the Kabala but the Catholic religion preferred to hide it, for they knew that if everyone *remembered* it they would not need the church but could find God on their own. The

Be and it will Be

Jewish religion did this too. There were many rules and regulations, which prevented certain members of the community from learning the Kabala, and it is only recently that it has become available to everyone.

You see, the Kabala is not a religion it simply *is* All That Is. As I keep saying there is no right or wrong - each choice or experience belongs to the *one* alone. Let me ask you how you feel about people who know that they are dying and there is no hope? Are they allowed the choice of opting out, as in Ethan's case or by euthanasia?

The choice to live and die the way he chose was chosen during his teenage years. In his case, the only way his choice could have changed was if a change of wavelength could have occurred by an older soul showing him the intensity of love which was missing in his mind and which he required. But this did not happen and so the story is written.

Don't confuse Ethan's choice with God's choice, which is what Ethan would have liked you to have done. This was Ethan's way of justifying his choice. The drugs were a direct choice of the way he was thinking, which was to be self-destructive. You see, the only way he knew how to attract attention was by rebelling - it was his payback for not having received the amount of love he thought he should. This does not make him right or wrong; it simply is the way *he* felt. The choice of suicide exists in God's world; otherwise he could not be All That Is. However this is not the recommended way to leave this earth and in "normal" circumstances there is always a choice. In his particular case and stage in life he made a wise choice. He now has an opportunity without body to think himself out of this wavelength of destruction. Sooner or later this would have happened, whether through a natural death or a suicide - he had nowhere else to go.

Zach: I am suddenly aware that I'm actually trying to make you say that suicide is not a good solution for anyone who feels that life is too hard for them. But you don't.

SOL: Let me ask you Zach, have you really got in touch with your feelings? Have you asked yourself if you are for example *angry*? You see, you have feelings concerning this experience which you have not yet fully come to terms with. You will find out eventually that your need to know *why* comes

Be and it will Be

from the fact that you have not yet accepted that everything in your life is a result of years of conditioning, ending up in judgment of others.

You are not individually God on your own, but are God altogether and the fact that God created this choice is simply a fact and there is no room for judgment. You see, being non-judgmental means not judging another's business. It is that simple. Everyone has a psyche and everyone operates from a place within themselves. And no one is perfect. Therefore, in order to get to the place of serenity through being non-judgmental and being accepting of others, one must first have compassion and understanding that, like you, no one is perfect. You see, there is no price to serenity - this is the ultimate state of being - and I think that you agree that to have serenity is *bliss*.

Zach: Yes, I think that I have come to a point where I can understand this, at least on an intellectual level. If there is no right or wrong then obviously there is no room for judgment. I can also see that not judging and accepting that things are as they are can make our lives much easier, nicer and more interesting. But you see, here is the catch. Just saying what I have just said includes some kind of judgment and on the practical level it is very hard, at least for me, to avoid judging things as good and bad or better and worse, etc.

SOL: Hurray! You finally got it. This is what I have been trying to enlighten you with. You see, you are so occupied with your intellect that you refuse to see the truth about creation and that is that God only wishes for you to *enjoy* creation! There is no catch Zach – the fact that you think there is, is your way of not letting go of your mind. You still have limitations. *There is* a practical way of doing this and you have already gone someway towards this through affirmations and other changes in your habits. Do not forget where this change has brought you to over the last few months. This is your choice to do or not to do. Rather than keep searching simply get on with it.

CHAPTER THREE

State of Being

One Month later

    Zach: Hey SOL, how are you?

    SOL: Always well, Zach - I am always in positive - I am.

    Zach: We ended our last conversation where I said that I could understand on an intellectual level that there is no good or bad and therefore no room for judgment. However, from my point of view I have certain preferences. I'd rather be healthy than ill, wealthy than poor, for example. Aren't these preferences creating a world of good and bad around me?

    SOL: Good or bad is not created by your preferences. There is no judgment, as these are objective labels which man has attributed to certain circumstances. It is your state of being that creates "good" or "bad". You were given the right to be and you have forgotten this. You are striving to get *there* rather than being here at this moment in time. You choose what you want to be at every moment. You are given opportunities in which you have to *be* through your choice to be. Good or bad is felt through being, through feeling, and cannot be measured by different objective situations. How do you know that being wealthy is better? There are many wealthy people who would disagree with you.

You see, it is not how wealthy you are, it is about your state of mind. You can be generous and poor or miserly and rich. Generosity is a state of being - it usually feels good. Being miserly usually does not feel good. Prove me otherwise. What I am saying is that the objectivity of all your descriptions is one big illusion - it is always only a state of your being. In fact, you can decide to be happy right now. You do not have to work at it or wait for it to happen. This is the key.

When you are happy you are on a wavelength that attracts happiness and when you are generous you are on a wavelength that brings you generosity, and when you are wealthy, in your state of being, this will bring you wealth. *Until you are you will not get there.* And until that time you will experience all other situations which you are being in your present state of being and this is what you call being in a bad situation. You manifest bad or good through your state of being. You can choose good all the time if you want to.

Zach: I must tell you that this is not as simple as you describe. I am unhappy and I would like to be happy. How do I choose to be happy? I mean, if I'm saying that I'm happy wouldn't it be some kind of denial to my present state of being?

SOL: Your *state of being* is a pre-sent moment through a previous *state of being*. This is the key, Zach - it is who you are at the given moment. I am not saying deny what you feel as it is the only way to *be* if you admit and respond to the moment. Doing this will set you free to *be* whatever you choose next. *Now*, I argue with you that it *is* very simple. You make it complicated. Let's go over this again. Recognize what you are or what situation you are in at a particular moment in time. Respond to it through a choice and set it free. If there is something you wish to attract to you, then after setting free the pre-sent moment, *be* in a state you wish for your self and this state will deliver to you another pre-sent moment based on this state of being.

Zach: It indeed sounds simple the way you describe it. Let me see then how this can apply to the current situation I'm dealing regarding my career. Up until some time ago I was "safely" working as a rooky lawyer at one of Tel-Aviv's well-known law firms. I am saying "safely" as it was exactly how I saw my life for many, many years and it seemed that my future was being built according to what I considered as my path. I was doing quite well as a young lawyer and even enjoyed the job once in a while.

This all changed when my good friend Ariel offered me a position in what seemed to be a very promising, yet risky, start-up company. It was pre-internet boom days and the company was involved with mobile email solutions. This proposition was risky for me, as I didn't even know how to send an email at the time, nor did I have a mobile phone! I can't tell you how difficult the decision seemed. I was raised in an environment where stability was the name of the game, particularly when it came to career issues. Both my parents had only two jobs in their lives in governmental positions where they slowly built their careers from the bottom up. For me to take such a risk at that time seemed quite out of context to my upbringing.

Quite surprisingly, they were both very supportive about this opportunity, but I had to go through some sleepless nights before saying yes. Eventually, I let the sense of adventure take the lead and within a short time I found myself in the uncertain situation of not knowing if I would be earning a salary at the end of the month. This position turned out to be very exciting and a lot of fun, but I always had the feeling that I couldn't really trust my employers. I guess that this was one of the reasons for Ariel and I to accept another offer that came a year or so later, which was the option of being a founding partner in a new technology joint-venture. That joint venture was a spin-off of a well-established company and we felt flattered that the owners offered us a significant part in this new project. We were both highly motivated and with the spirit of entrepreneurs spent days and nights in the planning and building up of the new company.

Eventually, we became disappointed to find that the information we had received was not altogether accurate and the people we were partners with, were not reliable. The development of the technology was not what we had expected and we began to have serious doubts about the feasibility of the whole project, and after two months of really hard work, we decided to leave the project and move on.

I would like you to show me how to apply what you say to this example, because after two months of working it doesn't look as if my wish is being fulfilled but quite the opposite is happening. You have suggested that this moment was pre-sented to me through a past state of *being* but I do not know how to relate to this. Please could you show me through this example?

SOL: Zach you are relying on your wishes and not on your state of being. As there is no real past it is your present *state of being* that is bringing you to this situation. I shall explain. Your state of being is who you are at the moment - how you feel about yourself. There are certain aspects of your *being* that can only be brought to conscious levels through the mirroring of others. This pre-sent moment is inevitable since it is a result of your state of *being*. If you were *being* reliable, if you were *being* self trustworthy - if you were *being the* person behind the wish for this moment to come out differently then it is that simple. Of course, in order to understand this you had to go through it, as it was a direct result of your state of *being*.

Ronny: OK SOL, it's me, Ronny. I have something I want to ask you. I want to be slim - I have been for a long time and I'm still on a special diet. What is stopping me from losing weight?

SOL: Hi Ronny, well first of all, your special diet has nothing to do with the amount of food you're eating. What is stopping you is the fact that you are not *being* slim, as you are afraid to say good-bye to that part of your *being*. As long as you are in the state of the *being* that you are in now, you will not lose weight. You have become so attached to your weight that you will not depart from it. When you are ready to depart from this state and without fear and *be* in another state, you will then have the pre-sent moment of this state of *being*.

Zach: Let's discuss "the person behind the wish" as you describe it. Does it mean that I have to be in a state of mind, as if my wish is actually fulfilled and then it is fulfilled? And if so, how can I really know what my state of mind is, as I've already learned that I am not always aware of it?

SOL: No, Zach, your mind can play tricks on you. *Being* is through, here it comes, your favorite, *feelings*! You *feel* your state of *being*. As with meditation, this is not a technique, it is a state of *being* where your whole body is the meditation. Being rich, being generous, being kind, being loving - this takes over the whole of you - your whole self, including higher and upper body. That is higher power and lower earthly body. Your whole self is *being* the thing you are. If you wish through your mind only, then you are in a state of information - speculation – unknown. If you *are* one with your body, you are manifesting your wish by *being*. This is a physical dimension and everything has its beginning in this thought, which is manifested into your state of *being*.

So no, you do not do "as if" although this can bring you to the *being* state as you will have begun and triggered it, but go beyond "as if" and simply believe you are.

Zach: This isn't clear enough for me. I can relate to what you say as far as meditation is concerned, although I can't really explain it in words. I just know that when I'm truly in meditation (what I call "a good one") then it is something I feel all over my body and therefore this is my state of *being* as you call it. I do not know how to explain how I got to this state of *being*. Please expand your explanation using a practical example such as how to transform into a wealthy state of *being*.

SOL: You have all been conditioned to relate to objects that you require in order for you to be happy, such as money. I say that it is not the object that makes you who you are, but your state of *being* that brings you to the objects. So you will not have money unless you are in the state of *being* wealthy. *Being* just is. When you first came into this world you were in a state of *being* of who you are in the purest of forms. Through conditioning by your parents and society you forgot how to *be*, but instead adopted roles to play in order to survive.

What I am saying is that you do not have to play a role in order to get there but have to go back to being that pure speck of creation which can *be* anything it wishes through who you really are. When you realize that you are creation itself, then you will be able to be who you wish to be. For example, when you first meet a girl and wish to impress her, there are times that you are actually someone else for a few moments whilst changing into that person you wish her to see.

You see, you have all *beings* inside of you and simply have to bring them out. *Being* is not something to strive for. It is right now in you and is waiting to come out.

CHAPTER FOUR

Practicing the State of Being

One Month later

    Zach: Hi SOL, how are you feeling?

    SOL: Hi Zach, I am passed feeling - I AM. Thank you.

Zach: You are passed feeling? I'd like to go over that, too. I, as you know, am not passed feeling - in fact, I have spent some time during the last couple of weeks practicing what you have suggested as a method to change my state of *being*. According to what you have said there are three steps: 1. Recognize who you are at a given moment - this is done by feeling who you are. 2. React to what you are, this means letting it go if you don't like it. 3. Change your state of being by feeling that you are what you wish to be.

I guess my first question would be - have I really practiced what you suggested?

SOL: Well, first things first - I do not feel because I am not in a confined body and therefore I am in a no time zone. Therefore, I am in *love* - in *knowledge*. I therefore do not have to feel - only to choose. And yes, we will go into this further.

As for your understanding of the steps - you are correct except with step 2, I suggest that you *act* and not *re-act* as if you are meeting something for the first time.

You see, react is re-act. That is you bring into the moment a past reaction. Treat each moment as if you are experiencing it for the first time. This is what is so exciting about life. As for having practiced this, you have understood it on an intellectual level but you have more work to do in the sense that when you ask yourself who you are at any given moment, you must recognize the feeling that is underlying "the who you are" and where that feeling is coming from.

Always ask yourself if this feeling is true. Most feelings about who you are come from what you think other people think of you and this is what you have to let go of. It usually has its basis in childhood. You have all given permission to others to dictate to you who you are, and others have never been your gods. No one is to blame, this is simply what you call conditioning.

Zach: You have indeed mentioned some of the problems I encountered while practicing the steps. The first, one of the basic problems, however, is that I sometimes find it hard to believe that it is really working this way. I mean, it looks too easy although it's not. And because I do not know people who change their state of *being* in this way, it is also influencing my confidence.

SOL: The fact that you see this as a problem is already a hindrance. This is not a problem but a key to a healthy way of life. And yes, it is easy, you only have to do it to believe it. I have said before that seeing is believing; "Na'ase Venishma" (the Old Testament says "Do and you will know"). In the physical dimension there is no other way but to experience in order to gain the knowledge that this is true. Oh, you can try and say that this does not work but you cannot know until you try. This is my argument to you — now prove me wrong. Many people know this. Some even practice it. You may even have read books by some who teach this. Of course, it is a choice, Zach. You can either carry on as you were or endeavor to find a new *modus vivendi*. The simple truth is that all God ever wants for you is to experience a joyful life through a happy state of being. This is the wavelength to good creation which means choosing positive thoughts which puts us on a positive wavelength and brings good experiences into our lives.

Zach: Well, God and I have something in common. I, too, wish to experience life joyfully through a happy state of being. Therefore, I accept your advice. I will not mention the word "problem", but there are things standing in my way to practice these steps.

One of the obstacles is that I'm not sure that I always recognize what I am feeling and I am not always aware of this. There are so many kinds of feelings that I'm not sure if this method applies to all of them. There are emotions such as happy, sad, angry, hurt, etc. There are physical feelings such as headaches and other physical pain. You have also suggested

Be and it will Be

that conditions can be felt such as being wealthy and I'm not sure I understand what it means to "feel" wealthy. I'm sure I have not covered the full list but these are basic to me. Please explain.

SOL: Let's put these in some order. First of all, you and God want the same thing. The only difference is that God IS already and is not in the state of wanting and you use your *Ego* to fight what *is* rather than really accept it. In fact your main obstacle is your *Ego*. When you find yourself in a certain situation, first accept it, as there is nothing you can do about it. Secondly, the feeling of who you are at the moment is how you are re-acting to it.

Are you angry? If so why?

Has the moment offended you in any way?

Is your re-action appropriate for that moment?

Are you reading the moment as it is?

Where is the anger really coming from?

This applies to any feelings that trigger your re-action. Remember, re-action means you are re-acting to a feeling that is surfacing as result of a past re-action. It may have nothing to do with the moment.

Now, physical pain is not emotion, however emotions can derive from physical pain. What does the physical pain make you feel - are you afraid, angry? Does it make you feel less of a human being compared to others? Are you enveloped in self-pity as a result? You see, physical pain can result from emotion which can manifest itself physically. All in all, if you have obstacles then simply remove them by first recognizing what they are. Where is their source? And ask yourself what you gain from keeping this feeling, which is a result of a thought which is not necessarily a fact. Of course, this may all seem cumbersome at first but the more you practice the more it will become second nature. You will eventually be in God's will.

Zach: You are right. It is indeed cumbersome, at least at the moment. If I understand correctly you are referring only to emotions as the key for changing a state of *being*.

SOL: *What else is there?* It is how you think of yourself that brings you to your state of *being*. Do you love yourself - are you deserving? Do you trust yourself - can you rely on yourself? All this and more bring you to your state of *being*. I have a test for you. Take tomorrow and decide that whatever obstacle you come up against you will accept it as it is and deal with it in that manner without emotional re-action and see whether your day will pass smoothly. If you put joy in your response to the moment, your day will be enlightened. Try it and you'll see.

Zach: Okay, I'm willing to take this test. I just want to see if I understand it correctly. I can decide, for example, that I'm not getting angry whatever happens - as I have done so in the past when I was working as a flight attendant.

When I started that job I found it very demanding and quite annoying. I had to work for very long hours serving people in a confined space, serving people who treated me as if they owned me. I used to spend most of the time standing up, sometimes on a 12-hour flight, and all the time follow different service tasks. The supervisors were, in many cases, at least as tense as I was and this sometimes resulted in an unpleasant atmosphere. I'm sure that any waiter or flight attendant can easily relate to what I say. The problem was of course that I really needed that job at the time, as it was a very convenient arrangement for my university years. I could arrange the flights in a way that did not conflict my law school schedule and the job supported my financial needs very well. I must admit that I did enjoy flights to a foreign city, staying in New York, Amsterdam, or Paris as it was really a nice break from my usual life at those times.

I realized that since this job was very important to me, I had to find a way to make it more pleasant. My solution was not to get angry or annoyed during those flights, whatever happened. This was not a conscious decision and I convinced myself that whatever annoying and unpleasant task I had to do, it didn't really have anything to do with *me*. I remember that some of my colleagues used to ask me how I managed to stay so calm and cheerful during those exhausting flights and I would simply reply that I don't let anything get to me. And so it really was – whatever happened I never got angry. Thanks to you though, I have learned to get in touch with my emotions and this puts me in a different position now.

Also it is quite different to decide "not to get angry" as a flight attendant, where nothing really touched my life, it doesn't happen too frequently, however, sometimes I just get angry - I mean I have no control over it, it just happens, especially when the weather is very hot. You will probably say that it is mostly about my Ego and I know that it is, but what I would like to understand is how to implement your method in such cases?

SOL: Have you heard the saying, "Rome wasn't built in a day"? You are a perfectionist, Zach, you want to be God himself in the purest sense and I shall let you into a secret - you are. However, you chose together with God to be embodied on the physical dimension and there are rules to abide. First rule is that learning is a result of time and action. So yes, you will come across these states of being all through your life but I assure you that with action and perseverance you will be in a much healthier state of *being* than you are now. Now, as for the weather - this is an external condition and I say that there is always a choice for how to make yourself feel good in a given situation. First accept it and do not fight it but do not use it as your excuse for getting angry. It is not the weather that is making you angry. Let's be precise; it is making you uncomfortable or rather you decide to give it power over you. But most of all, Zach, do not berate yourself for not reaching perfection. After all, this is one of your major lessons - not to be so hard on yourself.

Zach: Am I still so hard on myself? I thought I have let this one go. You see, I am not always aware of who I am. And by the way, being angry is not my dominant state of being, but being fearful is. As I have mentioned before, this is something that just happens to me and I don't always know where it is coming from and why. I mean, sometimes it even takes a while before I realize that this hollow feeling in my chest and my stomach is actually an expression of fear. In other cases I only know that I feel emotionally bad about something and I am not even aware that I am in such a state. I have to admit that I have learned that in these cases I usually escape by smoking a cigarette, eating a candy, or watching an inane television show to avoid these negative emotions.   What I'm trying to say is that I do not always recognize the "who I am" in a given moment and even when I do, I do not always recognize the source of this state of *being*.

SOL: No state of *being* is a bad state of being. There is no reason to judge it that way - it simply is. Fear always comes from a state of being where you contemplate a future – that is an *unknown* state of *being*. This is pure conjecture and a waste of energy. When you really understand that living is only done in the *now*, you will not be in a state of fear. The source of fear cannot always be recognized in the particular moment as your action is being decided then. It is alright to tackle this at a later stage too.

As long as you recognize it - this is not something that you will be able to do and know overnight - it will take time but being aware will already bring you one step closer. The thing is, Zach, that what I have been trying to explain all along is that you have the ability to respond to a given situation and that is All That Is required of you – that is your only responsibility - all the rest is beyond you as Zach.

CHAPTER FIVE

Thoughts and Meditation

2 months later

    Zach: I keep getting this feeling that I knew you when you were Solika and that I was the one offending you. Is it true?

    SOL: You feel that way as it is true. But you did not offend me, you actually tried to help me but did not succeed and that is why you are feeling guilty. I remember you well, you were a friend of the family and knew what was going on. But by the time you arrived it was too late.

    Zach: Please tell me all about it. I feel very strange right now.

SOL: Well, when you realized that I was to be kidnapped since my father refused my marriage to the prince, you arranged that I would hide in a friend's house and you left me there with a woman in order to go back for my father, but by the time you came back for me the prince's friends had found me and dragged me through the streets until I died. I had stones thrown at me. You know now that there is a tomb built for me in fez where Muslims and Jews come to visit and that is where my body as Solika is buried. The Prince's father had the tomb built out of feelings of guilt when he was on his deathbed. I suppose that I did not die in vain... A little humor on my part!!

Zach: Wow! This "previous life" business is astonishing and I would like to investigate it a lot further, but I believe it would be better to deal with this present life first.

SOL: You have had many lives, Zach - this is just one of them - and they are all happening right now. I will explain. Re-incarnation does not happen back and forth, it happens in parallel worlds. In fact, scientists who think that one day there may be time travel are looking in the wrong direction. What they should be concentrating on is quantum leaps.

You see, the dimension you are in, or every other world is in is linear. They go forward. The fact that there are other parallel worlds allows for other probabilities. In this world your father is your father and you cannot change that, but in a probable world your mother may have married someone else and you may be having a different experience over there. Also, if you were a Viking in a past life then you really are one now in a parallel life. This is a much easier concept for scientists to pursue and if they placed their energy in the right direction they would in time be able to get a glimpse into this. I agree, let's go into what we call enlightenment of your present life, as this is what we want to pass onto others.

Zach: I feel a little stuck today, as if my mind is loaded with too many thoughts. I often find myself preoccupied with my mind. I drive my car and about a zillion important matters are crossing my mind back and forth, and without any real purpose. Whilst I'm taking a shower my mind is busy with all tomorrow's "ifs" and "maybes" and I don't really pay attention to the shower itself. These are just a few examples and

Be and it will Be

I am really getting tired of this pattern. Is there anything I can do about it?

SOL: Meditate regularly and clean your thoughts. Enter each day with a clean mind and know that everything you are seeing is for the first time. Be in the AWARENESS and not in the thought, which is fantasy. Be in consciousness and aware at the same time and not in your re-actions. Be aware in every situation as to what your re-action is and why it has come up. What is it about the situation that has brought about this re-action? Has it really anything to do with the moment? This is a process that in order to get it to be second nature it has to be practiced every moment. This is discipline. Do you think you can last a week like this - not being in your head but being in the *now*?

Zach: Well, here I do understand what you say on an intellectual level, but I'm not sure how feasible it is for me. I mean, to avoid thinking in the manner you suggest sounds quite difficult. I do understand however that this can be very effective and I would therefore like to get a more detailed explanation as to how to do it. How about we use an everyday example to illustrate this further?

SOL: Easy. First of all I need to stress that this can be done and is being practiced by a lot of people. I mentioned a week because if you take a week to do this you will bring yourself to that level of training where it will become easier every time you do it, as you will have experienced it and experience is *knowledge*. Let's take a day in the life of an ordinary person who gets up in the morning and goes through whatever they have to do to get themselves to work.

Have a look at what happens when you first open your eyes - all the feelings that you go through. I don't want to go to work today, I'm too tired, I can't face that person today, etc...

All the thoughts have to do with *yesterday* - they have nothing to do with the *now*. Now, this is a new morning, there are new things about to happen this day, none of which have yet been discovered. Maybe with a clean slate you will not feel so tired. Maybe you will feel like going to work, maybe that person won't even be there or may have changed their attitude. You just don't know - you are already entering the *new* day with yesterday's feelings and

Be and it will Be

yesterday's thoughts. My suggestion would be to focus your attention on the *now*! Brush your teeth *now*, pee *now*, dress *now*, go to work *now* - notice what you see on the way *now* and so on and so forth. By the way this has nothing to do with creative ideas, which are also thoughts too. You see, when you are in the now, your creative ideas are even better as they have a clean venue. Did you get the gist of what I mean?

Zach: I believe I did. Actually, it relates to your previous advice - do everything as if you are doing it the first time. I did as you suggested for sex the other day, and boy, what a great experience it was!. When I do remember this and imagine myself as if it's the first time with my girlfriend, this is when I'm experiencing the greatest lovemaking ever even though we have been together for quite a long time. But you see, here is the problem. Usually, when I wake up in the morning, and this may be only me, my mind is exploding with thoughts. I don't know how to really describe it, but it is as if so many machines are working together in this little head of mine. So I take a cigarette and relax for a while.

What can I do instead - I mean practically do?

SOL: Zach, meditation is a very practical way. There is a meditation technique that specializes in getting to that mindless zone. It is very simple and requires concentration which in itself is meditation. Concentration = meditation.

All it is, is focusing on something or not focusing on something. Can you see that this is the same? Anyway, you just sit still and breathe deeply three times - inhaling and exhaling. You bring your energy from the top of your head by imagination down to your toes and back three times. You then sit very relaxed, and each thought that comes into your head you say, not this thought, not that, not this, not that, until you get to a point where there are no thoughts. *Silence.*

This of course does not happen overnight, Zach. It is a training that takes time on your zone, but once you have reached it you will be able to access it freely and easily. I have said before that there is freedom in discipline. If you get yourself into a regular routine of meditating twice daily you will get the hang of it. This all has to do with awareness. When you are in the awareness you are in fact relaxed and cannot be stressed. When you are stressed you are in fact not you but something else

Be and it will Be

possesses you. You see, it is all about who or what has the power. If your thoughts have power over you then you will be stressed. If you have the power over your thoughts then you will be relaxed. Simple, ha!

Zach: Well, sometimes it is very simple and I feel "high as a kite" in those few precious moments. However, sometimes for example, I become very anxious. This is when without any notice my mind goes wild with thoughts of all kinds, mainly worries or things I want to happen right now. Just a few days ago, I couldn't pee for almost half an hour because I couldn't get myself relaxed. And I was aware that the thoughts were not real and that if I could just get into silence everything would work out. But I couldn't do it, I just couldn't.

SOL: You didn't want to. This may sound ridiculous to you but I say that it is true. Sometimes you get into that state of being and you do not really want to release it - it is like an addiction and I know you will find this hard to accept but I tell you this is true. You see, it would mean that you would have to say goodbye to that familiar part of you. The way to get out of it, by the way, is to first of all breathe. This is a very easy thing to do which you have all forgotten. You all breathe under your breath and the air is in fact your life channel. But let me say, worries, anxiousness, whatever you wish to call it are still all thoughts and the way to release them is to become aware of the reality of your situation.

When this next happens, stop and look around, see the reality of your situation and ask yourself what is the hurry? Ask yourself what would happen if you stopped being anxious? Ask yourself - here it comes - who really cares whether I am anxious or not? Who am I anxious for?

Zach: I know you are right, but thinking of what has just happened or what might happen seem inevitable. It's not that I want to run these negative scenarios through my head but they keep coming and coming and it can take time before I realize that I'm experiencing this kind of a negative mind trip. What is your advice to help me when this starts happening and what would it take for me to realize when this is happening?

SOL: Again, Zach, I say meditate regularly. It has taken you twenty-nine years to get to where you are and now you want to master everything within a few seconds! You need to train your mind to let go of the thoughts. The more you train the more you will be aware when this situation comes up. This will get easier with time. The thing to do is

Be and it will Be

to not give your power to the situation but to keep your power and observe the situation. This way you will not be in the thoughts but out of them. You will be an observer of a play rather than a participating actor. In this way you are in control. Try it, it is a great game! I do it all the time.

Zach: Sometimes I do try it and it works, but then I suddenly get very afraid when I find myself in this kind of silence or find myself in a place where I am watching myself from the out side. I mean, one moment it feels very pleasant and the next moment I feel fear enveloping me. Why is it so? And what should I do when I feel this fear taking over?

SOL: Zach, you are afraid of the unknown. This is an unknown state of being for you, but it really is the safest place as it is God's. You see, you are used to being in control. When you are out of thought you are actually in the process of *surrender*. Surrender to the *now* is surrendering to God. God is the now. It is all very simple and you need to *trust* that you are safe.

CHAPTER SIX
Practicing Meditation

One Month Later

    Zach: Hi SOL. Any suggestions for starting this one?

    SOL: Hi Zach and Ronny. Well let's go into how you have been doing lately with meditation - this is something we should talk about a bit longer as it is the essence of how you can choose to deal with life in the physical realm. It is your umbilical cord to All That Is and when you are not connected to All That Is, you get lost.

    So my suggestion is to work along these lines. When you meditate you enter into silence. This is your connection to God, everything divine. Therefore, your physical entity is not your true self.

It is this realm of silence, the connection to God which is your true self. The reason for stress amongst most of you is the belief that your physical identity is your true self and thus there is conflict. If you have the belief that you are God and have control of own life, and when matters do not happen as planned, then you become frustrated. When you are connected to the true SELF, the God self, and realize that God is the true ruler, that's when you have peace.

Do you have any more questions for now?

Ronny: SOL, I need clarity on the subject of control. On the one hand we are told to create our own world with our own thoughts and on the other hand we are told that God is the creator and the results are in his hands. So, which is it?

SOL: Both are correct. You see, when you are connected to the source you are God and therefore have the ability to create your own world and at that moment when you are connected you are with God and with all creation. What I am saying is that when you remove *Ego* and allow *God* in, you are the biggest creators of all time because it is God who is creating, which in turn is you. And this is for the better good of all, as when you are connected you are *all*.

Zach: There are many things I'm not sure I understand here. First, the issue of God. We have been talking about God quite a lot and I don't know – maybe it is my religious background from childhood, but I must admit that this word scares me a bit and talking about it scares me even more. You see, I have grown up under the impression that God is some kind of a master judge who is watching everything that I do and deciding whether we go to heaven or hell accordingly. My understanding was that the Jewish religion had very specific rules about what pleases God and what makes him angry and I remember, that I was constantly afraid that I would do those things that God didn't like and get punished. As I write this down it all seems very shallow and childish to me, but I was a child at the time and these were my beliefs about God.

As I grew up, I remember it was at the time of my Bar Mitzvah, the day when a Jewish boy becomes 13 and therefore liable for his deeds in the eyes of God, when I decided to rebel. I'm not sure why I made this drastic move, but I think that from a childish point of view I couldn't really accept the doctrine that stated that God is the Almighty and at the same time is so demanding. I mean, why would someone or something that has all that power need somebody else to please it, and then punish them if they "disobey" him? I know that religious people would say that you have to follow those rules for your own good and not just to please God, ridiculous as it may seem, but I was not willing to accept that theory.

I thought that if almighty God gave me a mind to think and make decisions, then I should use that gift to determine what is good for me and what is not, and not be occupied with a set of old rules to follow without any consideration. I was young and probably somewhat arrogant and stupid and I took it to the extreme, doing things you must not do, according to religious practices, just to see what happens as a result.

Even though I became a religious rebel, I was still very afraid of what God would do to me for my misbehavior. For a long time I would think that anything unpleasant that had happened to me was a result of a misdeed and I am not sure I am utterly over that state of mind which was rooted in me from a very young age. Through my teenage years and onwards I have learnt that the term God is perceived in many different ways by different people, and therefore I find it important to make it clear in our story what we mean when we use the term God. What *is* God?

SOL: This is the question which has been asked most throughout eternity! And yet look how many people on earth are religious – how many speak God's name.

It is very simple. God is *you* and you are God. There is ONE THOUGHT- ONE ENERGY, which is divided into physical realities and non-physical non realities and they are all One. Divided and undivided. You do not have to go far to reach God as *you* are part of God – God is *within* you. It is that place where the Ego leaves that you can find God. It is *Creation* itself. It is the thought that creates the table and chairs you sit on. It is the lightening in the sky. It is the creation of the tree. It is everything and everyone - IT IS. The fear you talk about comes from not accepting these facts as true and instead developing theories outside yourself that create untruths, and these are what you fear. How can you fear the truth? The *now*?

Zach: If God is all there is, what exactly is Ego?

SOL: God is ALL including the Ego. Everything ever created is God. The Ego is a defense mechanism built in to protect you in the physical realm – such as when crossing the road and being careful not to be hit by a car.

Unfortunately, the mind, which can be your own worst enemy, has given the Ego too much power and allowed it to take over your life in areas where it should not. In fact, the Ego can become the devil itself. This is and always has been the invention of the mind - again which is also God.

Are you confused yet? Let me elaborate. You see, the non-physical realm is everything you ever thought of. It is God not energizing, if you will. It is God's thoughts. In order for his creations to see and meet with reality he has had to have every single thought. How else can you *know*? How else?

So the mind is God and the Devil derived from the mind is also God and all is God and you have *free choice*, which is of God. *That is how it is.*

Zach: So is the Ego meant for just keeping us from physical harm and does it become the "devil," like a bad servant when we over use it? How is the mind related to the Ego?

SOL: The Ego was built in creation for protection mainly from physical harm and sometimes from spiritual harm. For example, when you know that you are being wronged by another. It is like an alarm system. When you become arrogant you misuse it. As with anything else you have been given – for example you have all been given power and energy – if you combine power with Ego you try to control others but if you use power without Ego you can actually serve and help others such as healing. You see, anything overused is abusing your gifts. Ego is in some aspects a gift and in other aspects it is abusive. It is all a matter of which focus you give it and your attitude is. It all boils down to *choices* as to what you do with your gifts.

CHAPTER SEVEN

The Ego

3 Months later

Zach: Hi SOL, it's been a while since we last spoke, but I have been practicing some of your suggestions quite intensively over the last few months. I still have quite a few questions regarding the Ego-God duality but before we discuss that, I would like to get back to meditation and share with you some of my recent experiences:

I have been practicing meditation on a daily basis over the past three months and I think I am onto something. Let me know if I'm going in the right direction. Sometimes, whilst in meditation, I can ease the stream of thought and I have found that your suggestion, "not this, not that" helps a lot. Thanks a lot! Then I can feel beneath my belly the presence of some kind of energy within me. It is a little difficult to describe but to me it does not feel like a physical presence but more like a silent energy that feels both warm and pleasant. I have been practicing meditation occasionally for more than two years now and I have experienced this kind of feeling before, but it has now become more intense and I sometimes have these pleasant feelings when not in meditation when I go through my everyday life. In these moments I just focus on the lower part of my belly and there it is. When in deeper meditation, I can feel this energy throughout the whole of my body.

    I have noticed that different parts of my body might be stiff, for example, around my mouth, my forehead might be tight, my shoulders pushed upwards for no specific reason. It seems that these areas within my body have been like this all the time and I just haven't noticed it before. Sometimes I have let this energy flow through these different parts of my body and eased them, bringing them to relaxation. At other times it just won't work. Now, this is what bothers me…. unfortunately there is always something that bothers me! Do I feel what you referred to, as God? Is this true, meaning this is not an illusion? Please elaborate as much as you can and please tell me what else could be gained through meditation?

SOL: God is everywhere - you are God at all times. The feeling you feel during meditation enhances your connection to God and opens the avenue to God. Meditation is the best way to connect to the purest of energies on the highest level and of course it feels pleasant. I will explain. As you already know, everything and everyone is God and God is the creator - the creator of Ego, also.

For it is with and without the Ego that you come to know God. It is after discovering the duality of the Ego that you find God. How else can you understand the relativity of matter? So in meditation you can connect to that same place where you become one with God. This place is the truth that underlies the Ego... i.e., you. When you are more in tune with this space you can become more objective in your ways and thus rely less on your Ego, as you will know the truth behind it. You are energy, but because of Ego and daily will, you forget the truth which is always there underlying everything else. So in order to remember, you meditate. Finally, you will discover that true control is beyond your body and is of God.

There is a grand design and everyone makes the mistake of deciding your lives rather than discovering it.

Life is happening whether you like it or not - it is a continuation in a timeless zone. This is very difficult for you to fathom, but once you realize that the only control you have is over your thoughts, which result in your reality, you will know to change them accordingly, and know that God is taking care of the results. Even if the outcome may seem unfair – the outcome is there, as the underlying thought you have is to learn a certain lesson and this lesson is brought to you. It is a pure manifestation of the energy thought, which is God in the first place. So on the mundane level - ALL IS ONE and ONE IS ALL and yet you can only *be one* at a *time,* tuning in all the time through meditation in order to discover the reality of your life, for it is this reality which will set you free.

Lots of love, SOL

CHAPTER EIGHT
Desire and Let Go

2 months later

Zach: Before we start today, I wish to share with you quite an extraordinary experience I had a few nights ago in Toronto. It was the last night of a relatively long business trip and I was quite homesick. I was flying across the US back and forth, trying to do the best for my company before going back home, and by that I was quite weary by all this traveling and was eager to get back. I spent most of the trip meeting new and unfamiliar business counterparts and I felt somewhat lonely on that particular night and went to bed in this rather negative mood. I woke up in the middle of the night as I had had a dream of a character of someone who seemed somewhat abnormal. His name was Danny. From this dream-like state I understood that he had channeling capabilities somewhat like Ronny so he would be able to answer my questions by channeling SOL and he would do it the same way Ronny does, by writing the answers down. I had no particular question for him but I just had this feeling that I was meeting someone who channels. When I woke up I had a very unusual feeling which is hard to explain. It was as if some kind of energy had entered my body starting from my head and going right through my entire body. It felt extremely warm and pleasant, somewhat like being saturated with love. And for no reason I started crying or more accurately my eyes filled with great volumes of tears.

It was a very, very pleasant feeling and somehow I burst into tears in an intense way that I have never experienced before. This was very unusual for me, as I very rarely cry. It usually takes somebody to die before I can cry and here I was, crying a stream of tears which I couldn't control. Boy, what an astonishing experience that was for me. Not just the crying, but mostly the feeling of a presence of this energy within me. I had no idea from where and how it was coming, but I didn't really mind as it felt so safe and pleasant. I can only describe it as a "divine" feeling. Since in a way, SOL, you were part of this experience and since you are the closest thing I know to divinity, I couldn't help wondering whether you were involved in this. Was it you by any chance?

SOL: Yes, I paid you a visit.

Be and it will Be

Zach: That's all? Come on, give me some more details.

SOL: It was just a reminder that you are connected to ALL THAT IS and that you have to adopt the habit of total trust.

Zach: All right, you have satisfied my curiosity but I can tell you that you are most welcome to visit me any time. Now, back to our conversations. Something crossed my mind about the Ego – God duality which we have been discussing. Correct me if I'm wrong, but my understanding is that God is everything and thus Ego is one of its aspects. It somehow seems to me that you're kind of describing a good guy – bad guy scenario, where the Ego aspect of God is the bad guy and the pure level of God is the good guy. What do you think of this?

SOL: Good and bad is something that you interpret. I don't use those terms - it is much simpler than that. There is only relativity. The introduction of Ego is the relation between the individual and the environment, whether physical or metaphysical. How else can you know the difference? When the Intelligence, Universe, God, All That Is "decided" on a physical dimension in order to find out who God was, God brought about the Ego. Otherwise there would not have been a separation in which God would have been divided into billions of particles. There would be no way of knowing who God is through all those different mirrors without Ego because then there would be no way of measuring anything. So in fact Ego is the door to relativity and allows for all the lessons and knowledge on the physical dimension to come about. Imagine life without relativity – it would all be "sameness." In fact there would be no *life*. Ego is *life* on the physical dimension. But here it is – you have all misused it and tried to control life through it, while its true role is open the door to relativity – that is all. God and Ego are in every human being, the human has the Ego. The *being* has God which In Hebrew [Nefesh Chaya] means "Living Soul."

This is the makeup of a human being all in one. When you deny one, the other suffers and vice versa. If you give too much to the body, the spirit (the God in you) suffers and if you give too much to the spirit, the body suffers. So all in all as I mentioned earlier you do not have to be perfect but you should strive for balance. Ego, by the way is not always bad, it is sometimes a protection. So to sum up, in some experiences the Ego is good as you say and in others, bad. However, at all times of life, which is usually impossible on a human level, even the Buddhist monks have minor problems with this, the ideal is to walk with God every breathing moment.

Zach: I guess it all boils down to what serves us and what doesn't. What makes us feel good, healthy, peaceful, etc., and what makes us feel bad. And again, if I understand you correctly, walking with God as you say, should take us through the first path and make us feel good.

Now, here is the most fundamental problem, how do we know which is which? How do we know to distinguish between God and Ego? When we realize that this is Ego, how do we know if it serves us or not?

SOL: *There is no serenity or peace with Ego.* Think to when you are very excited and on a high as a result of something that had elevated your Ego. Can you also feel peace with that? Usually when it is Ego there will follow an anticlimax and reduction in energy. When it is God there is a safe feeling of peace and serenity. This is the difference. You see there are no highs and lows with God. It is always here and now. There are no highs and lows in here and now. The Ego is a result of the lower *you* – the one who is fighting to prove who you are on the mundane level but this is never who you really are - it is the actor and not the real thing. That is the God underneath.

Zach: So again, how do we know which is which? There are so many voices from inside and outside telling us what we should do in a given moment. Let's say that I'm willing to let only God direct me, how will I know to recognize God's directions?

SOL: You will know. It comes from the place behind the Ego. Always ask yourself, do I have serenity and trust. The choice is always yours. It is your free choice and God will not interfere with that, although you can seek his answer in the silent state of meditation. Most of the time the answer will be to go with the flow and perhaps not to take action. Sometimes not taking action is the same as taking action. Everything, whether done or not done, results in something. Sometimes you also have an underlying thought, which is your intuition. You are not aware of this most of the time because your Ego brushes it aside. When you want something really badly and your intuition says no, your Ego will make sure not to give it power. So if the world which you create happens to coincide with your intuition you act surprised and say, "How can this be?" You see, sometimes your intuition can actually save your life. I will explain. Sometimes it may seem that this underlying intuition is not good for you but after some time passes you can see that this is what was meant to be.

In fact, Ronny has a great example of this. Remember, Ronny? You were asked to sell your apartment and even though everyone advised you against it you had an underlying feeling that this is exactly what you should do. Looking back, is there anything you regret? Would your spirit be in a different place now had you not have sold your apartment and allowed that "turmoil" that accompanied this change in your life to take place? So you see, your Ego may have thought that it would be best not to sell but that little voice which advised you to do so has taken you through the most incredible journey of your life.

The intuition is your *gut* feeling - you feel it in the stomach. Literally. If you develop your awareness in this area you will see that this is the case. It is a message which is relayed from the left side of the back of the brain (from the same area where Ronny channels) and it is sent through the nervous system to your gut. That is the place also where you feel *fear*. That is because fear is a warning. It does not mean that you should live with it, it means that you should be aware that something within you is not balanced. If you were balanced you would not feel fear. When you feel fear in the same place as intuition you cannot be aware of the intuitive thought as it is covered up by fear.

Zach: What do you mean by saying that trust is for the results and not for the choice? Do you mean that if I'm following God's directions, assuming that I can recognize them, then the results will be those that I can feel good with?

SOL: This is very simple - the choice is yours and the result is God's. The trust is the knowledge that whatever the result is, it was meant to be and rather than fight it, accept it, so that you can go on to the next level of experience. The serenity comes with the acceptance of the moment – of the result, which is God's. It is the fighting for the

Be and it will Be

result that brings the Ego into action. *Let go of the fight and the Ego will vanish.* Results are facts – they simply are! The sooner you all realize this the sooner you will flow with God. Remember the equation - Creation + Free choice = Knowledge. This is all there is to it. Very simple!

Zach: I totally agree that once something has already happened, the best way to deal with it is by accepting it as a fact. But you see, we are all messed-up with Ego before the result stage because we are afraid from certain outcomes. Let's face it - disasters are happening all the time on this planet. People are getting hurt in many ways, physically, mentally and emotionally and it happens all the time. All we want is to avoid those results and thus use our Ego to prevent them.

SOL: In most of the situations you have described these things happen because of *Ego*. Human beings are running on Ego – once you get into the mode of being ruled by Ego you do not know when to stop. And this causes others to act with Ego and retaliate.

Take car accidents for example – if everyone drove the way they are supposed to without Ego, there would not be any accidents. Think of the different moods you are in when you leave the house in the morning. On one occasion you will be serene and allow someone to cut in front of you and on another occasion, when your Ego rules, you will do anything not to allow that person to overtake. Hunger is a result of Ego – politicians have to answer for this. There is no reason for anyone on earth to be hungry. Believe me, there is plenty to go around. How many meals can you eat a day? How many millions of dollars can one family need? This is all Ego and greed. Oh, *I am not saying that you are not entitled to plenty*. What I am saying is that these are people who can change the world and instead they use their Ego and greed to get more for themselves rather than share for the better good of all.

Zach: Let me then ask you this straightforwardly: If I'm following God's directions, if I live the here and now all the time, can I trust that I will be safe? Can I trust that I will avoid these daily disasters? Can I trust to be free to do all those things that I desire to do?

SOL: You are free to choose to do whatever you like every minute and second of your day. The results of your choices are God's but the choices are freely yours. Trust and safety mean that you understand that you are God. You are *energy*, so whatever the results are, they take you go to God. The kind of trust and safety you seek are those of the Ego – they are the results that you wish to have, such as being wealthy and healthy. God gives you what you need to learn and not what you want. Your trust in him has to be total and accepting of whatever he brings you. This kind of TRUST gives you the feeling of being safe. For example, say you are on your death bed, this will require a great deal of trust from you to know that God is doing his best for you. You may say that your best is to stay in this dimension and will not understand that God's best intention is that you do not remain. Not asking *why* is total *trust*. I realize this might be difficulty for you but your wanting to stay when God wants you to go, is the Ego fighting God. There are occasions when the God within you really wants to stay and that is when God cooperates.

    Zach: Excuse me, but I have to argue something here. I find it hard to agree that we have an ultimate free choice as we are very limited in many ways. An extreme example is that I am unable to fly. A more mundane example is that I cannot afford a new Mercedes. What do you say about this?

SOL: I say that there are two kinds of free choices, one of the Ego and one of God. The Ego wants the Mercedes and God does only if the Ego is removed. You forget that you are God and actually can fly. Your energy can leave your body under certain circumstances and in fact, Ronny has had this experience. This experience is even better than any bird's. But yes, on a more mundane level, as you are in a body and in a relative world, you are in fact limited.

However, within this confinement there are many choices. Allow me to remind you that the free choices I refer to are spiritual. They are the choices that decide for you how to live your life on earth and which are your priorities. Are they of Ego or of God's? If they are of Ego, you will be running after the Mercedes. If they are of God's, you will be asking and receiving serenity and maybe the result will be a Mercedes!

Zach: Why is a desire for a wealthy state of being of Ego? As I see it, it is only a desire for independence.

SOL: The desire itself is not necessarily of Ego, it is what is behind the desire. If the desire is for self then it is for Ego. If the desire is for the better good of all, then it is of God's. Again, how many people do you know who are wealthy, and although they have economic freedom, they also have serenity? Serenity is a commodity that has no price. It is the most valuable commodity there is. If you are wealthy and have serenity then you have it all.

CHAPTER NINE

Letting go of the Ego

One month later

    Zach: Hi SOL, I would like to start this session by telling you that my Ego has been very active in these past couple of weeks and although I recognized this, I have been unable to let go and I have felt frustrated most of the time.

    I think it might be because we are going through a very difficult time at work. We are currently trying to raise funds for company growth and after working with a group of potential investors, suddenly there has been a big change in the US stock market, which is now going through a huge slump, generating a great deal of confusion in the industry which I work.

    The group of investors who had already agreed on certain terms for their investment in our company, are re-

Be and it will Be

considering their investment and have backed down. Two weeks ago we had high hopes for our company and now its very existence of our business is in danger.

Of course, on a personal level, I now find myself in turmoil again, and as much as I tried to implement the practices and meditation to find serenity and acceptance of things I cannot change, it isn't working for me, and in fact, I have found myself overwhelmed with a sense of failure again. As I said, frustration is the best way of describing the way I've been feeling in the past few days.

SOL: Zach my dear, Ego is part of you and this is something you have to live with. The important lesson is knowing when to and when not to use it. You are not perfect as I mentioned before, and this is why you have chosen this dimension. Even the "holiest" of people such as priests have to deal with Ego on a daily basis. This is just how it is. It is very rare that a human being is able to live without Ego at all times. In most cases the Ego is there to protect you and you have to distinguish when this is so or when you are manipulating its use beyond its purpose.

The first thing to do is to stop criticizing yourself, and accept yourself every day. What I am trying to teach you is how to live in the physical time zone. That is being here, in the now at all times. I realize that this is difficult but it is the purpose of living.

Zach: This is something that I find difficult to admit, but the recent events in my life bring up one of the emotions I really don't like about myself and that is jealousy. So, how would you suggest I deal with this? It happens to everybody I know that we want what other have got and we become jealous when we can't have it. I may be childish and spoilt but this kind of thing makes me very frustrated.

SOL: We have discussed this before and I know that you will agree that the most important thing to achieve is personal serenity. We also discussed that peace and serenity are derived from acceptance. Acceptance of the moment. The frustration you feel is Ego manipulated and is a result of the fact that you do not accept the moment. Remember, the moment is the result of a previous belief and therefore the time zone relates to *this*. There is a timetable that belongs to the universe - the universe is all energies together on a higher level which results in your beliefs.

Be and it will Be

Therefore, in order for something to inspire you, you must first accept the moment and change your negative beliefs, as these will not bring you the things you are looking for. The universe may decide to give you your request or desire in another ten years from now. What will you do, be frustrated for ten years? This is what I have been talking about. *You cannot desire and hang on to that desire at the same time - you really, really have to let go of it to allow it to happen.* And you are definitely not letting go.

Zach: So what you say is "ask and you shall receive" but only if you let go of that wish and not necessarily on your timetable? I definitely agree that I don't let go. It is difficult for me even though I'm usually aware that this *is* the time to let go. Even when I say to myself "let go" and I mean it, it is not always happening.

SOL: You have to stop talking and start doing. Remove the Ego in the instance and give it to God. Allow God to take the place of Ego. This does not mean that God will give you the thing you desire, it means that God will give you the serenity to wait for the things you desire to come to you.

Also, you should always remember to desire with the better good of all in mind. When it is solely for the self there are repercussions. Letting go Zach, is much simpler than you think - it is a state of being. You relinquish your need to be in control of the situation and allow the Universe to take over instead of expecting the results to happen in the way you wish.

Zach: Do you have any idea how difficult this is to implement as a human being? And by the way, you said earlier "don't criticize yourself too much" and I'm trying to do this too, but it seems like there is something built into my personality which stops me.

SOL: To your first question. I have all knowledge because I have experienced all. So yes, I do know. But I also know that this is a secret to a good wholesome life in your dimension and this is what I am passing on to you.

You humans are bound by too many chains and they are usually physical. Your concept of feeling limited actually results from the fact that you limit yourself by binding yourself to many mundane matters and physical structures.

Criticism is not built in; it is a conditioning which you have adopted from your elders. You behave toward yourself the same way in which your elders behaved toward you, and therefore you can decide to get rid of whatever binds you. This is your world to create and only you can free yourself.

Zach: Sometimes my belief system is actually working against my desire. For example, I feel somewhat guilty about my desire to be wealthy. What do I do in this case? How do I know if my desire is for the better good of all?

SOL: First things first, Zach. Feeling guilty is the same as not believing that you deserve, so in fact you are giving the Universe double messages and the Universe cannot take the command. So get rid of the guilt!

The point here is for you to understand that you create your world with your beliefs, but the results of your creation are of the universe and of God's so that you have no way of knowing the exact outcome. Yes, you can desire and let go the desire and the creation may come about but not necessarily the way you had planned it. You see, this is the secret - do not write the script, just give the desire of how you wish to *be*. The Universe will take from its "files" and compile the picture. This means that you have to totally trust that God is doing for you that which you cannot do for yourself.

So you see we are back to the equation - Creation + Free choice = Knowledge. The creative desire and thought is yours. The doing is yours. And the rest is God's the way God sees fit. Just accept it, that's all!

Zach: What about *my* desire and the better good of all?

SOL: If *your* desire is pure and you know that in your heart you will be helping others, then this is something the Universe will take into account. But Zach, this is what is important and I want you to listen carefully:

It is your state of *being* that is for the better good of all. You have quite a way to go spiritually. You see, anyone can be wealthy, but if their state of being is not high and pure then their money or wealth will not be for the better good of all because, very simply, money is energy and is a magnifying glass, and if there is evil then this will be magnified and if there is good then this will be magnified.

I hope you understand what I am passing on to you. It is not the fact that you have money and wish to distribute it to others. It is *how* you will distribute it and what people will receive from your *being*.

Zach: Am I not a positive *being* as I am now?

SOL: You are positive but Ego is still very much in the way and we did say that we are expecting Mastership! So I suggest that you learn to let go and know in your heart that you are on your way to a higher plane of spirituality and the rest will come.

Zach: Okay, this is in fact what I really, really want. Is there any "homework" I should do until the next time?

SOL: For the next week let go. Do what you choose to do out of the moment and let go of the results, knowing that the results are God's. We have gone through this before but this is the only solution. Look at the reality at every moment and accept it and make your choices out of that. Lots of love, SOL.

Zach: Thanks, SOL! I love you too. Now, regardless of all this, can you tell me what is the sharp pain I feel deep in my belly and how to let go of it and what is the cause of it?

SOL: *Fear* and *anxiety*. If you follow through this week as I have suggested this pain should disappear. Let go of the control and allow matters to work out the way they are supposed to. Let go, Zach. Let go!

Be and it will Be

CHAPTER TEN
Taking Responsibility

6 months later.

    Zach: Dearest SOL, it has been quite a while since our last conversation and this was a significant time for me. I have just got married! This has been the most exciting event in my life. I have brought this up as it closes a circle with my relationship with you and it shows how your spiritual guidelines actually work.

    My first question to you when I first met Ronny about four years ago was about my inability to maintain a healthy relationship with a woman. Since then I have been on a spiritual journey with you, where I have learned to get in touch with my emotions and to allow myself to "feel".

    It is very difficult for me to admit, but my greatest fear about relationships was rejection. That is why I preferred to take advantage of my good looks and sleep around with as many women as possible, never allowing myself to become attached to any of them. Through this process with you I became aware of these fears and slowly developed the willingness to let go.

Looking back, it is very clear to me that I met Tal, exactly when I was ready to start a new approach. It was the first time that I allowed myself to love someone before making sure that they loved me first. This was definitely a new level of trust for me. This change in my life is so dramatic that many of my closest friends are still surprised that I have decided to choose this path. Some of my male friends still refuse to believe that I can be satisfied only with Tal. The future obviously is unknown, but I sincerely hope that I will. Tal is the most wonderful gift I have ever received and I feel very lucky to be her husband. I truly believe I met my soul mate and I am full of gratitude for this.

Tal and I have just returned from a trip to India where we had the most fabulous honeymoon. I don't know what it is about that country, but it brought us both closer to our higher selves. We have had many exciting adventures and the peak was our meeting with an old German woman in one of the isolated beaches of Goa. It was very close to the end of our tour and by that time we were both very serene and feeling very connected to our higher selves. Neeru, the German woman we met, was quite extraordinary and on a very high level of awareness.

Be and it will Be

We were discussing mediation and she suddenly said that there is *nothing* really and *everything* is actually made of that same *nothingness* as she called it.

I was already familiar with this idea – as an idea – but I wanted some further explanation and asked Neeru to elaborate. Neeru said that this wasn't something to explain in words but something to experience. As I was very curious, I immediately asked if she could let us into such an experience. She was silent for a moment and then she said that we both seemed ready for this. We then went onto her balcony, which had a marvelous view of the beach, and sat silently for a while. Neeru then asked us to "expand" – simple as that … It is very difficult to describe what I felt, but I definitely felt larger than my body. It was really something extraordinary! I felt as if my physical body was only a small part of my being. At one point I focused on a nearby coconut tree and I actually felt for a short time as if I were that tree. This went on and on and I felt bigger and bigger and then I believe I got a glimpse of what Neeru said and for a very short time I felt that there was indeed *nothing,* and at the same time I was *everything*. Boy, what an experience! One I will never forget.

A few days later we had to leave those wonderful beaches and come home. It was very difficult to get back to a "normal" routine after that amazing honeymoon and I experienced the most terrible toothache. Since I feel a little uncertain about that experience I would like to get your point of view about what it was. Is there something I can do with this?

SOL: Dearest Zach, welcome back! You and your wife have had a spiritual awakening which will bring you both to a higher spiritual plane. Your reunion as two commuting souls has brought you to this level. It is one that you will experience both together because you are a couple and each separately as an individual. You have experienced creation in the knowledge that ALL THAT IS - is! Whether you are a tree or an insect - you are always God in his creation. When you look at the insect, you are in fact the insect, as you have created it. If you do not see it, it does not exist. This therefore may be a little difficult to fathom and this is the area of quantum physics, but you see, you create and then you witness. Nothing exists beyond your creation! This was the point of this experience and you will get more familiar with this as time goes on.

You ask what you can do with this. Well, I believe that you are in a new position of authority at work. Therefore, you are in a position to bring people around you to a higher spiritual plane. You are not in your working environment for self only but to help others see the light. In fact, I suggest perhaps you could introduce a course in meditation for all those who work with you and thus improve the energy around you. You will also have ideas of your own I am sure. You are probably already playing with this idea and asking yourself how you can suggest such a thing or go about it. Well, my answer is that when you really believe what I am saying as the truth you will do it.

As for the toothache, you have come down after a high in India and in order to bring yourself back to "earth" as it were you have chosen to experience some sort of physical tangibility. But what you may have wanted to experience through this pain is the use of tools you learned or discovered in India and thus really know that"this too shall pass". This way you would not have given the pain too much power, but you would have been a witness to it.

Zach: Funny that you mention my promotion, as I was about to bring this about next. First this was a surprise to me. Around six months ago I told my boss that my expectations were to become vice president at some point. But we never really set a date or an event upon which this promotion would happen. Therefore, it was quite a nice surprise when I got back from my honeymoon and he invited me to his office to tell me about the promotion. I felt very flattered, yet one of my immediate thoughts was that now I would have to bring more profitability into the company. In other words, I feel now some kind of pressure as I have much more responsibility in making this company more profitable.

SOL: There is no difference between now and then. The difference is that your employers see in you that this is what you are capable of and therefore have trusted you with this promotion. You see, Zach, when you plant the seed of a tree, the tree already exists in that seed. You have the power of creation in you as you have always had, and now the time has come for you to bring this creativity out of you. Trust in your creative Godly powers, but also remember the importance of what I mentioned previously, about helping others to improve their creative godly energy in your working environment. This will help bring new projects and new business about. They will do it and you will be the one motivating them.

Zach: What about the need that I feel that I have to work harder now and spend more hours at work due to the new position? Spiritually I believe that I am actually working too hard and should spend less time at work and use the time for other purposes.

SOL: I have one thing to say to you: quality not quantity! You have been promoted because of your capabilities and not because of your time. Time is not a measurement for bringing good business – you know more than anyone that sometimes you can strike a good deal in one conversation which takes no more than five minutes. So get rid of the guilt which is holding you back and concentrate on what really is important.

You see, actually if you read the last chapters you will see the connection. Even today's session connects to the last one, where we spoke of Ego. You see, if you were not so involved in your Ego you would not have had to ask the question about how much time to spend at work. It is your Ego that is worried about what the others will think now that you have been promoted and therefore you think that they are expecting you to put in more hours. So mostly we are working around how to get rid of Ego in order to really live the life that is meant for you.

Zach: You know, this is very interesting! We have been discussing Ego in one way or another ever since I was lucky enough to meet you. I have always understood this on an intellectual level and in India I also had the chance to really experience what you call Egolessness. I spent some significant time at a Meditation Resort in Pune and the awareness was very profound there. Indeed, all through that trip this awareness was guiding me and it was amazingly wonderful. I was really living in the moment, at least most of the time! And look at me now - so little time has passed and I have gone back to living with Ego so easily. I even find it a little difficult to explain to myself the distinction between the "Ego me" and the "Godly me". Can't you live life in the western, industrial, business world and at the same time live an Egoless life?

SOL: Zach, Zach, Zach! You are a child – you are still learning! First, not everyone who lives in India is Egoless! Don't forget that you were in environments in India where you were being taught Egolessness - even those teachers themselves find

Be and it will Be

themselves in situations where their Ego is very dominant. The fact is that you are on a journey of knowledge and that you are aware of this Ego situation, the more you are aware and the more you practice the more you will get a hold of it. Do not be too hard on yourself. You have arrived home to your familiar surroundings, and old patterns are difficult to get rid of. Think that all through your years of growing up you have trained yourself to think in a certain way and now within a few months you wish to change everything you ever knew. Well, it can be done and knowing you, it will be done, but be patient with yourself, or rather, let go! *Know* deep down that the *lesson* this book is teaching is about the Ego and now you have your new position which will bring you fulfillment. This is the way that the book is developing and you are beginning to understand it.

Zach: So please remind me again: what Ego really is, how do we get rid of it in our daily life, and what do we gain out of it… a typical Ego question I guess?

SOL: Ego is a self-defense mechanism – it is there to protect you when there is a life-threatening situation, or any threatening situation. However, you all misuse it. When you come across any situation, what you really need to know is that you have the responsibility or the ability to respond to that situation by simply trusting in your Godly self. There is no need for Ego. When you use Ego only, God cannot be in the picture. God has given you this mechanism for spontaneous reactions that will help protect you, such as in accidents. Here the Ego is at its best. However, in most situations the Ego gets in the way and "Edges God Out". In your daily lives it is advisable to look at situation objectively, where you can witness what is happening and thus rationally act upon it through knowing your abilities – this way you will not need to use the Ego.

CHAPTER ELEVEN

Serenity

Two months later.

Zach: Hi SOL, I've run out of ideas as to how to continue our book – how do you suggest we go from here?

SOL: Well dearest, we are still on the Ego subject. As you may have realized, this is the key issue of the book. Now is the time to talk about the theory which you have so eagerly related to everyone around you. You and Ronny have each been able to put this theory of letting go of Ego into action and since it is very easy to sink into old patterns, this is something you should keep practicing every day so that you get it right and can be an example to others. After all, you do want people to believe in what you are preaching?

Zach: This is exactly what I had in mind. Do you suggest then that we pick on some of the issues in our lives and see how we can practice and implement what we have learnt about Ego?

SOL: Great minds think alike! Well, just before you go into examples, I would like to remind you of the theory that applies to every aspect of your lives.

Remember, the reason you are on the physical dimension is to experience through choices, one experience at a time. So with that in mind, know that in order to proceed to the next experience you have to leave the old ones behind. Remember also that each choice of experience has to be for the better good of all. Since everything works on wavelengths in this universe, every choice is important because if the choice is for self alone it will backfire. Also note that each experience and thought will have brought along a feeling and an emotion which will have turned into a belief, thus entering your belief system. If you remember that you made a choice, then you will also know that you can change the belief. In order to change the belief you first have to recognize it and then let it go. You can then jump into the new experience without fear because if the choice is for the better good of all there is no need to have any fear because it is of God.

Zach: Okay, but one clarification before we proceed as I'm afraid that many people will feel guilty after reading this. There are different ways to perceive "the better good of all" and I know some people will exclude themselves when they think of the better good of all. You once told me that sometimes the better good of all starts with the better good of self. Please explain this.

SOL: Here we go – we are back to the Ego as promised. You see, the wanting of a new experience through the Ego, through the wanting for self alone is not healthy. Let's go back to the commandments - *love thy neighbor as you would love yourself!* You see, Zach, this is the whole theory in a nutshell – you cannot love your neighbor if you first do not love yourself. Yourself Egoless – yourself being serene and loving and only wanting good. When you have this you will automatically want it for others since serenity comes first – it is of God. Think of a situation where you have made it – with all your riches and yet the people around you have become resentful of you. Then there is something here that you are not doing. You see, if you really wish yourself well then you will not want resentful people around you since they will remove your serenity.

So the point of this is that when you have those things you wish for because you have learnt to love yourself through God and the Universe and without Ego, you will also wish to share this good with others so that there will only be good energies around for your serenity.

Zach: So if I understand this correctly, then it would be love yourself first and only then love others in the same way. But if you don't love yourself in the first place then you are not even able to love others. And if you take care only of yourself, then you won't be able to be serene, as the negative energies that are the result of such selfishness, will not let you be serene, right?

SOL: Sorry, Zach, but you still have not yet got it. Selfishness is self with Ego. I am speaking of self without Ego. Think of your higher power or what God would want for you. God would want you to first be serene and for you to be comfortable, right? How else can you give what you do not have? If you wish your surroundings to be serene then first you have to be serene and then people around you will want what you have. How else can they see what they want from you? Hence the better good of all.

Zach: If I understand you correctly then our main objective is to find out how we can be serene and this should automatically lead to the better good of all. Have I got it this time?

SOL: I was just going to say, *by golly he's got it*! You see, take a situation where you wish to do several things. You have a lot on your agenda and you have to give your full attention to it all. It is very difficult not to get yourself uptight and when you do this, nothing ever goes right. But if you first have serenity, believe me, things have a way of working out. Appointments get cancelled or postponed or you simply know what to do. When you are serene – that is with God - you are able to be focused. You see, you cannot listen to two songs at the same time. Right?

Zach: This may sound dumb given all the many sessions I have been through with you, but this seems quite revolutionary to me! You see, you go through your life thinking that you have to make money, be healthy, find the right partner, etc. – all in order to eventually be serene and here you say, be serene and then everything else will work out for you.

SOL: Yes! I say have a God in your life rather than an Ego and you will have serenity. What is God if not serenity - which is the Universe. It is that knowledge that shows the way it should be. I am offering you the key to your wishes. I am saying, *be with God*, have *serenity*, and your wishes will come to you with no effort. Of course you understand that when you have serenity you are actually changing your belief system and it works when you work at it. So this is it, Zach – you have hit the jackpot!

Zach: Do you have any idea how difficult it is to really believe in this very beautiful theory? I mean, there's some kind of a Catch 22 here. I believe that most people will find it very hard to believe that if they focus on getting serene that everything will work out for them.

SOL: Zach darling, this has long ago stopped being a theory. Many have put this into practice and it manifests itself daily. You do not have to focus - you see this is the surprise. You each have it in you since each of you is God and God is serenity. You simply have to release the Ego and let God surface. *This is not something that takes any effort - it simply is a State of being.* All the twelve-step programs promote this. They have all understood that no one can wean themselves off alcohol or whatever else without serenity, simply because the Ego wants the substance but God does not. So this is not a new invention, but people on the whole have not been open enough to accept this into their lives. I seem to remember a young man who once said he wishes to be *cool* and I said *be* cool- *be serene.* You see, what use is it if you have all the things you wish for if you are not serene? In fact, if you are serene you have it all!

Zach: So what do you say to all those people who would say we couldn't be serene just like that – we first have to get this and that in order to be serene?

SOL: Again, everyone can have serenity since it is in everyone. Very simply remove Ego and you have serenity. Live one day at a time and you have serenity. Remove the wish to control others and places and things and situations and you have serenity. These are all wishes of the Ego. Simply be who you were intended to be. Use your ability to respond through your free choice and be serene in the knowledge that you have done your best with Ego or judgment. Simply *be*!

Zach: But we are afraid to simply *be*!

SOL: I have news for you- you *are*! Anyway, the only difference is that you are afraid. Remove the fear and you will *be*.

Zach: Okay, so let's get practical with this. What would you choose as the first topic to deal with? I have many topics running through my head things like health, money, relationships of all kinds, career, etc. What would you pick?

SOL: All topics actually fall under relationships. You see, in this dimension you have a relationship first with self and then with the outside world. There is nothing outside of you and everything is self-referral, so when you say money I say relationship with money. When you say health I say relationship with health. You see, all is in effect of how you conceive your relationship with SELF. If you are afraid or resentful or whatever, you will come across this in all your relationships. Take the example of money – you may be resentful that others have more money than you and therefore you are not being able to receive money or keep. This is the result of the way you conceive it. Serenity is something that solves all emotions and all matters or patterns. When you have serenity what you are actually saying is that you are letting go of old ideas and allowing the Universe to take care of matters for you. You see, the Universe will answer your wishes if you let it. But if you wish to control the situation you will block the universe's efforts.

As for health, the same applies. What is your attitude to the health, for example? Since you know by now that recovery depends on your will to recover and the person – doctor or healer - can only assist if you allow them. When you have serenity the channels of healing are open. When Ego is in the way on either the part of the physician or the patient recovery will not be one hundred percent.

Zach: Okay, so what is your practical suggestion? You know I can be too logical at times. Do you have a list of action items?

SOL: First and foremost, and this was channeled to one of your world leaders, may I suggest the *Serenity Prayer* which I mentioned before. This is something that if you read it carefully clearly defines what is yours and what is not yours. You see, when you come across a situation that concerns you, you only have the ability to respond to it by your own free choice. The rest is none of your business. As soon as you have responded the Universe must answer in kind. This certainly removes from your shoulders a huge burden since you are then relieved of the control. In fact, remember to always relinquish your control to the Universe in exchange for serenity. By the by, this will certainly relieve some of your shoulder pain, which often affects you.

Zach: Thank you – I'm going to start with this as my shoulder so hurt quite often. I am still amazed that you know this about me. How do you know that my shoulders hurt? It has became much more painful since I got the promotion at work

Be and it will Be

and after reading what you have just said, I can clearly see the link. To adopt your suggestion requires plenty of courage as I see it. I am currently facing a situation where a major deal has been delayed. I have done everything in my ability to make it happen and if I'm following your advice, I should just become serene, let the universe do its part and the deal will happen if it is meant to be. This is a very difficult approach for business people in this world, as many of us grow on a "make it happen" philosophy, in the sense that we think that we have control of the results, and this actually means control of other people and if we don't "make it happen," it means a failure. But you know me. I'm going to do my best to implement this in my life. Especially on the career side where it seems that my toughest challenge is of relinquishing control while my boss and the company shareholders seem to care only about the profit. Looking rationally on this though, the wise choice seems very clear and even obvious. You can either do your best and be serene or do your best and be in stress.

You mentioned a leader getting the serenity prayer by channeling, who was that leader by the way?

SOL: One of the United Sates Presidents. Research it yourself as it will give you a deeper insight of this man and why he brought this serenity

prayer wherever he went. Lots of love and serenity,
SOL

The Serenity Prayer

God grant me the serenity to accept those things I cannot change;

The courage to change the things I can;

And the wisdom to know the difference.

CHAPTER TWELVE
Thoughts Management

Two months later.

    Zach: Hi SOL, I was giving a lot of attention recently to your advice about being serene in the face of events we cannot change, and while I still believe it is a very wise advice, I still find it very difficult to implement. Particularly as the situation in the company is very shaky and our ability to survive is questioned again.

    Therefore I would like to start with a different approach today. I know you never tell me the future, but I'll ask my question anyway and see how you choose to handle it. What is the future of the company I work for? I'm so tired of all this uncertainty.

SOL: Zach, you forget that you chose this uncertain world. Do you wish to give it up and to come and join me up here? I think not. Well, in that case you are simply going to have to stick to the tools and discover your life. You will see that you will be led to where you have to be. That is the whole point of your experience.

Zach: But I wish to win for once – I mean this is the experience I want to choose.

SOL: You choose the experience, not the result. What do you think winning is? Do you think that when you have finished your time here that your maker is interested whether you earned enough money for the company you work for or whether you have bettered yourself? Remember, you are he and he is you and all God wants is the best for you on the *spiritual* level.

Zach: But hey – you say we are here to experience and I simply wish to feel/be in that experience which is winning. Not for whatever happens after I'm gone, but like a football player who wants to score. I mean, I see them running so madly excited after scoring. I wish this to be an experience for me.

Be and it will Be

SOL: So be in the state of being which feels as though you are winning, Zach. But remember Ego. The winning has to do with the Ego, especially the one you are talking about. If you choose to be wealthy simply because you wish to experience having money then *be* there in your state of *being*. But you see, you have climbed the ladder of wealth and you forgot where you came from. You see, when you live the goal you miss the experience. Why are you not experiencing your good fortune *now*? You are always wanting more success and more winning. You see, you have won. You affirmed, did the work, and won but you are not satisfied. You will always want more if you do not appreciate the *now. This state of being* will bring you goals.

Zach: This is very true and I'm a little ashamed now. But you see, when I come to you, in this form at least, it is usually with my complaints and troubles. We humans, as you call it, tend to call on God mostly when we have some problem we don't know how to solve. Still, I'm consistently using one of the first pieces of advice you gave me before we started this book and that is thanking God for everything I have in my life. I do it every morning at the beginning of my daily meditation and I am glad to say that this thank-you list grows all the time. In fact, I actually prefer the relatively small steps in climbing up, spiritually and materialistically, as it lets me experience every step to the fullest. What is my problem then? Why – every now and then – do I become so eager to have more? Why does all of this at the same time also make me feel so guilty?

SOL: Zach dearest, first – choose *not to feel guilty*. That is yours to do. No one is forcing you to feel it! You are human and one of the human traits is that you fall into patterns again and again until you release them totally. So this is up to you. You see, growing up, the human mind is like a sponge. You adopt thoughts that belong to older humans around you and then you reach an age where you realize that you can and have an ability to think for yourself. But you see, as with a computer, unless you delete the old, you cannot put in the new since it has to take the place of the old. Where are you going to put it? This is also a matter of trust, when you trust your SELF enough to know that you choose and decide what to think, everything else will fall into place.

Zach: Okay, so let's take the issue I started with as an example. I was brought up with the thought that I "always had to be better". My parents, my teachers, my friends, and the circumstances I was part of have always encouraged me to improve - to be better than what I was. In every field – school, sports, social life – you name it. When I was six years old, in the first grade at school, my teachers decided that I could skip the second grade at the end of the year and go straight to the third grade. My parents' efforts to teach me reading and writing and some basic math at the age of four and five had created the desired fruits and at a very young age I was already equipped with all the skills that are required from a second grade pupil. I don't have any regrets about my childhood as there were many benefits from that situation. There was, however, also a downside to this as this created a lot of pressure on me to prove myself all the time – to prove, so I felt, that I deserved this class skipping. I remember very vividly one of my teachers in early third grade, telling me that they let me skip the second grade only because they didn't want me there. She was reacting to some typical childish misbehavior of mine, but at the age of seven I believed her and that sentence haunted me for a long time. Maybe even until today in a way, as I have always had that urge to prove that I am successful in anything I do, that I can score and perform and "show them" all that I am capable.

So here I am - never satisfied as you say - and if we keep to this logic, then I will never be satisfied as there is always an option to do better in everything. But you see, at the age of thirty, this is so embedded within me, how can I change this way of thinking, especially as everybody around me thinks this way. A good friend of mine asked me – if you don't want to be better all the time, how can you have the motivation to reach any goals or get anywhere?

SOL: Zach dearest. Who do you wish to be better than? You are an individual and your motivation has nothing to do with being better than anyone else. How could this be your gauge? Everyone is in a world of their own and all you humans should be occupied with is bettering yourselves for Self. There is no competition here since every choice you make is a choice made for Self. Each one of you has a handwriting that is very personal so how can you compete? Competing with another human being only brings out worries and depressions and relies totally on assurances from others.

Again, you see, we are talking about the Ego - it creeps in every time you are not looking. Remember, there is only one Zach in the whole universe and you are a copy of God as he made you. Why would you want to be better than someone else? How could you since there is only one of each of you? You see, there really cannot be competition because who are you competing against - God?

Zach: well, I completely agree with this. I guess that what I meant is not getting better than others, but getting better than what I already am. As you said about my state of *being* as far as wealth is concerned– I always want more than what I have and this is an endless journey and not just about money. What I am saying is that I was brought up with many people telling me that I'm not good enough, and therefore, this is what I think of myself – sometimes unconsciously – and this is very difficult to change.

SOL: First of all, wanting to better yourself financially is also based on the fact that there are others better off than you, otherwise, where would this thought come from? You live in a relative dimension and there is no way that you would wish things for yourself if you hadn't seen them elsewhere. How else would you know about it and why has it become so important to you? Imagine that you are living on a desert island where all you need were the fruits of the land. You would not be involved then in this kind of thinking. So it is still the competitiveness within you. Being not-good-enough is the pattern you have to work on to realize what are you really thinking i.e., not good enough for whom? Who is judging you other than yourself?

This is something that you can use the delete button on and replace it with a new thought. It is *simple* – just do it.

Zach: Delete in a computer is very easy. Delete the underlying "not good enough" thoughts and replace them with "good enough" is not as easy. Another thing is that I am not always aware of such negative underlying thoughts and then I can't even get to the delete part. As usual, my request would be for a practical tool – and I'm not underestimating the "just do it" – I'm just looking for the "How to."

SOL: Well, first of all, if you are going to replace a thought with another thought don't use a new thought that will limit you. Why "good enough"? Just "good" would be fine. Now there is another reference to your question of an underlying thought and this has to do with your *state of being*. When you have a conscious thought and want to have it created but underneath that thought lies one that says that you are not good enough for this thing to happen, it is that thought which will create or dis-

Be and it will Be

create. This thought comes from *who you are at this moment in time.* So if you are depressed or feeling at a low self-esteem, then this is what will dominate your creation. So you see, it is all about *who* you are at that moment. In order to identify the underlying thought in this instance you should tap into why you want what you want. You see, this is the paradox – for you to want something you do not have, means that you are not in that *state of being* that brings that thing to you. I say that it is one's *state of being* that brings your world to you.

If you are deserving of good because you believe that you are good and that this is your *state of being* then good will come to you. If you feel that you are non-deserving and that your self esteem is low then these things you wish for do not find their way to you. The tool is very simple – once you have recognized the negative thought, say to yourself, "I erase you now!" Do not give power to the thought - do not linger with it – do not turn it into a discussion. Simply *let it go* and allow it to leave the hard disc.

The problem with you humans is that you attach emotions to the thoughts and go through a whole separation as if you are losing a best friend. Well, in a way you are saying good-bye to a friend who in one way or another has helped you through certain times in your life. But you do not need that friend any more and it is time to say goodbye so that you can meet a new friend. Remove all familiar guilt feelings or nostalgic feelings that may align with this thought. It is actually a very technical thing you are being asked to do. So, let it be technical. That is why I say simply *do it*!

Zach: let me see one thing here. *Any* negative thought we have, we can just say "I erase you", and it will be gone? Does it apply also to the negative scenarios I sometimes imagine about car accidents, being fired, losing my wife, etc.? I mean, it sounds too easy and I admit I find it difficult to believe in it.

SOL: I repeat – do it! The second a thought enters the mind… stop it. It is easy. It is you humans who have made everything complicated. See, God gave you, *you,* one day at a time since there is no yesterday or tomorrow. So where are you living – in the mind? Or *here and now*? Which is the *reality*? Do you see how easy it is? You decide. You are in control of *your* mind Your mind is *not* in control of you. DO IT!

Zach: Do you realize that when you say "you humans" I feel somewhat inferior?

SOL: Who planted that thought in your mind?

Zach: Well… I guess I did. Now we are running out of time and I could continue this forever. So please just tell us how all this connects with the last chapter, which ended with using the serenity prayer as a first tool to relinquish Ego?

SOL: The serenity prayer is the delete button.

Zach: So technically, you suggest that we just say it whenever we remember it?

SOL: I say that you can *choose* to remember it. You see, with this prayer you actually go back to your creator all the time and allow him to bring the results. You relinquish the control and a great weight can be lifted from you since the only thing required of you is to choose and say the prayer in order to bring you to a higher spiritual lesson.

CHAPTER THIRTEEN
Managing your Feelings

Two months later.

    Zach: SOL dear, I have a few questions regarding the "delete" thing we have discussed last time. First, I must say that I have been using that trick quite a lot and I believe that it is working for me, especially for cleaning the "not good enough" place in me. I was concerned, however, that this tool would cause the suppression of thoughts and therefore place me in a state of denial. What I mean is that sometimes a negative thought turns into a feeling before I even become aware of it and I'm not sure that I can delete feelings. What do you think?

    SOL: Good question, Zach. This is exactly the place where you may get confused. You see, you cannot suppress thoughts, only feelings. If you delete a thought at the very early stage then there would be no feeling to suppress.

However, if you conjure up a thought, which already has a feeling attached to it, then this may very well be a feeling that has already been suppressed and is therefore being brought into the mind again. This is where you will have to do a little more work and actually recognize the feeling before you can detach yourself from it.

You see, it is only a feeling just as a thought is only a thought. The way you humans hold onto feelings is almost sad. There are feelings that you can choose to hold on to as they make you remember. Zach, the whole lesson here is to remember the equation CREATION + FREE CHOICE = KNOWLEDGE. What I am trying to explain is that you have a choice and you can decide each time whether to keep the thought or the feeling or whether not to. This is your ability to respond and therefore your responsibility. You can choose to stay on a positive wavelength or not. However, I do agree that where feelings are concerned that are beyond thought, there is a little more work to do. But ultimately, it is only a feeling. In order to depart from a feeing it first has to be *felt* as you cannot depart from an illusion but only from a manifestation.

Zach: So what you suggest actually is that when there's a negative thought entering our minds and this thought has already created a negative feeling, we should then just feel that feeling through – not try to escape from it – and at the same time delete the thought?

SOL: Yes, this is exactly what I mean. I do not, however, think that you should make this your favorite pastime – only when it comes up.

Zach: Do you suggest that this is what I have been doing lately? I mean I have this great challenge at work now and I find myself from time to time afraid of a failure. This brings a feeling that I well recognize, although I realize perfectly now that all those so-called "failures" that I went through turned out to be good things that happened to me after all. Still, that bitter feeling of a failure, of being "not good enough," still haunts me from time to time.

SOL: Zach, ask yourself what is "failure" – what do you think it is – what is your interpretation of it? As far as I'm concerned, there is no such thing as failure, there are only lessons. Your fear is an illusion. Oh, the feeling is real but that is all it is. However feelings are connected to energies. Yes, you are probably saying, wow, this is new! Well, yes, it is not the thought alone that is attuned to energies, but the feelings as well and when you are on a negative wavelength and feel for example, the *fear* then you project onto this wavelength and there is a probability that you will cause a fear to manifest. This is why it is so important to understand the ability you have to respond and choose. You see, God has created wavelengths. The whole of the universe is based on a wavelength. And this is how it works:

1) You wish something to happen in your life;

2) Choose a thought and imagine how it would feel

3) Physically make moves towards its happening;

4) The universal wavelength will meet you half way.

Amazing, isn't it?

Zach: Amazing is an understatement. I mean, come on. What about "do what you can and leave the results to God"? I though God is deciding which are the things that eventually happen to us out of our wishes. Here you suggest that we can actually get whatever we wish for.

SOL: Yes, but read number four. Number four is the God Result. You do what you can and leave the rest to number four. You are to feel the outcome in number two. I did not say that you will experience the same outcome but you will come close. You see, as you humans have not yet mastered this, then you cannot really reach the intended goal exactly as you expected. I have yet to see a human being who can delete all negative thoughts and feelings. Can you truly say that when you have intended something you have not strayed somewhere in the middle into negativity? A perfect example would be when you have decided to go for something but it has taken longer than you expected. What usually happens is that you lose trust and stop the wavelength. Am I right or am I right?

Zach: Right you are. As a matter of fact, I can say that this is exactly what I am experiencing at work now. Things don't happen as quickly as I would like them to and this is discouraging me. But isn't this inevitable? I mean, I need some positive feedback in order to move on with the same intensity and when I don't get it, it brings me down a little bit.

SOL: From where you wrote "Things don't happen…" to the end of your paragraph is a thought you can do without! Zach, you do not need assurances. You need intent and a belief system without doubts. You see you have made a statement which says *this is inevitable* and you chose to believe this. Choose to believe differently. You see, it is just a thought.

Zach: Well, this also requires a great deal of awareness, doesn't it? To have no doubts at all – is this human? Are we aware every time we have doubts?

SOL: It actually requires more practice than awareness. Zach, this is simple as I have said before. Doubts are negative thoughts, surely they can be recognized. I'll tell you what the problem is, otherwise you would not be arguing with me. You see, the problem is *trust*! If you fully trusted what I am saying you would simply do it but your mind takes over and becomes your enemy. Again, all God ever wanted for you humans, since God is in you, is that you enjoy the experience of life. The experience of life is in the creation – in the manifestation - and that is why he helps you when you help yourselves. Again, I suggest that you do what I say and then see if you want to argue. Test it for yourself for one week.

Zach: I will and I have and I believe my trust is growing all the time. The arguments are for those who don't believe – right?

SOL: Of course my dear!

Zach: Before we depart today, Tal, my dearest wife, [thank you for helping me achieve this beautiful relationship, SOL], wanted to know whether it was you or a spiritual guide like you communicating with her that night when she was sick in Barcelona. She had a fever and her temperature was very high and she was slightly delusional, but she heard a clear voice promising her that everything was going to be alright. Of course, she believed the voice was illusions brought on by the sickness, but the voice was still there.

SOL: You are welcome, Zach and remember that *you* made your beautiful relationship happen. Well, it was me and something else. You see, you may not believe this, but I am me and also you and God – I AM. I do not have an identity the way you understand it. I have the identity of SOL simply so that you can relate to me more easily. I am your higher power – the God in you – the last step before the CREATOR. *I am also the creator*! I go through a "*sieve*" if you like so that my energy does not burn you but I am All That Is!

Zach: Me too.

SOL: Quite Right! Lots of love, SOL

CHAPTER FOURTEEN

Getting Messages from the Universe

Two months later.

Zach: Hi SOL. let me start with some background before this new chapter. Last week I was in Singapore where I heard that the company I work for has probably lost a major deal, which I was leading. As you can imagine, I was extremely disappointed and called Ronny for some spiritual comfort. While we were talking she somehow went into channeling with you and you said that this was a minor thing and that what was really important was my spiritual growth. You said that when I am in foreign countries, it is always a good opportunity to be open to receiving messages that help our spiritual growth, and you suggested that I should be more attentive and listen to whatever comes my way. You also said that the spiritual growth would result in matters taking care of themselves also on the earthly level. So, the next day, I was very attentive. I read every sign on the street, I listened to everybody I came across, my colleagues, friends, taxi drivers, etc., until very late that day I talked with a friend of a friend and through that conversation she popped up a sentence: "I sometimes validate myself through my career." This was an alarm bell for me and it was immediately clear that this was my message, as in fact, I too, validate myself through my career. And I wasn't really aware of this until that moment. So, I believe I know what this means to me, but I'm asking you to elaborate on this and provide your clear point of view.

SOL: Well, Zach, you are right - this was the message you needed to hear at that time. First, allow me to tell you that there is not a day that goes by without a message for you. All you have to do is be objective and in tune with what is going on around you. You see, the way the physical realm works is that you are, or at least should be, attuned to wavelengths. The wavelengths are there and that is a fact. Only when you are in your head you are unable to attune yourself. You see, *life can be gone through effortlessly.* This is what I have tried to explain to you on several occasions. You need to use your free choice in creating your world but remember to use the results as messages too. These results are your signs of how to continue. Most of all, the more important element of why you are in the physical dimension, is to levy your spiritual awareness. Trust in God and follow him. And since he speaks through people, this is where you receive your messages.

You are who you are and your value of who you are has nothing to do with whether a deal goes through or not. But let me tell you that the deal can go through a lot better if you let go of control, which is total Ego. You are Zach without Ego – Ego changes you into something else and this is what lies behind the message. Life has many roads for you to follow and the place you are in at the moment is not your last resort. You have many, many opportunities that you can choose from and at the same time if you attune to your surroundings on a daily basis and listen to "God", the right message for you will arrive and you will *know* what to do. The result may not always be the one you expect but it is the result for *you* as it will lead you on your path.

Be and it will Be

So to sum up, what you need first is Trust in God and yourself and the knowledge that you can choose and use your choice freely, being aware constantly that life is *here* and *now* and not in the way you plan it in your *head*. Every maneuver you make leads to the completion of the puzzle.

Zach: Isn't it a little dangerous – to get God's instructions from "messages" passing by? I mean there are a lot of speculations and interpretations in this business and I know many people who say that specific signs mean specific things i.e., a broken mirror means a coming quarrel, walking under a ladder means bad luck –there are thousands like this. Also the daily horoscope can be considered as a message and we know how misleading and confusing this can be. Even rationality doesn't always work here as I have already learnt that you can assert two conflicting arguments where each relies on rational ground.

SOL: Zach, I am not speaking of messages that have to do with other people's minds. This is not being in tune with God. I said, if you read the previous paragraph, that you will *know* when the right message for you arrives, just as you did the one in Singapore. You noticed that when this happened it even had a higher decibel and you *knew*. That day you say yourself that you heard many people talking to you but that you did not pick up on anything. Well, why do you think you picked up on this one? Two reasons: the first is that you gave up – that is you surrendered and therefore allowed the wavelengths to work for you. At the same time, you had already planted in your subconscious that you were to receive a message. This is attunement. *You will know – trust me*. We are not talking rationality here – rationality is the mechanics of the mind and has nothing to do with the God messages.

    Zach: You are right – that sentence did have a higher decibel and as you say I knew right away that this was "my" message. I just know how people talk about "messages" and "signs" that at least to me seem false. So your answer is – you just *know*?

    SOL: Yes, you *know*. But let me elaborate even more. The messages do not usually arrive as advice but as a sharing of that person's experience. You see, that person becomes your mirror in that instance and when this happens there is no Ego involved. Because what turns a message into rationality is usually advice as the other person automatically, unless really low and humble at that moment, will not want to receive advice from another. So the messages arrive when your Ego is not involved and when the Ego is not involved, believe me, you will not go into rational dilemmas. But again, I say that if you are aware of how the universe works with regard to wavelengths then you will always know which message is for you.

Zach. Let me just mention that this *knowing* is relatively new to me as in the past and even many times now I have had many doubts as to what a given result means to me. As you said, results are messages too, so how do we work it out?

SOL: You simply accept the results as facts since that is what they are. You cannot argue with a fact, otherwise you will be in denial and thus this will undermine your capability of making a choice. How else can you go on to the next step?

Zach, it really is very simple but you are fighting with your mind, and your mind lives in fantasy most of the time. The real world is here and is made up of the consequences of your choice after the event. *You* choose. Something occurs as a result of the choice. You cannot proceed to the next choice without accepting the result of the previous choice.

Zach, you are not having fun. Everything for you is so serious and the whole point here is to enjoy the *doing*. That is the crux of the message. You see, if you were enjoying the process rather than living the results you would really get it. Life is a collection of experiences. Ask yourself "where is the experience?" Is it in the doing or in the result? The result, even though it may be a good one by your standards, will always be an anticlimax to the process. The results are your check points, they enhance how you feel about yourself and the message is to show that feelings are not facts. The result should simply be a stepping stone in the game of *life*.

Zach: Let me ask you something that a friend brought up when I told him about that message. He said of course you validate yourself through your career, otherwise, who are you without it? And not only your career. We validate ourselves through the way we look, how much money we make and have, how many friends we have, who loves us and the way they look.. and the list is much, much longer. If we take an extreme example of someone who is lonely, poor, homeless, jobless, etc. - who is this person – isn't that what we call a *nobody*?

SOL: Choices, Zach, choices! The poor person has a choice and is using it the way he wants to. I am saying that all the things you mentioned have to do with the mirror of the Ego, not of who you really are. I am saying that you can have all these wonderful things without Ego and even enjoy them more. But ask yourself who is behind the satisfaction when the deal comes through. Is it you or is it your Ego? If it is you without Ego, then that is the God in you, and you may be pleased on a different level. For example, you may be humbly pleased that you were able to secure jobs for people through the deal. But I promise you that your first reaction is the pleasure of your Ego. Yes, all your outside circumstances are reflections of yourself. But yourself in this case is yourself with Ego because you would not be needy of these things if you were attuned to the God in you.

I say that the poor man must sometimes even be on a higher attuned plane than you since he does not need to satisfy his Ego. Or then again, he could be the one who does not love himself enough and does not think that he is deserving. Either way, the satisfaction level that I am talking about has nothing to do with Ego, and I say that you can, and most probably should, have all the things you wish for if you wish them for the better good of all and *not* for personal satisfaction, which is where we fall apart since this level is where all you see is your Ego image.

Zach: We have probably covered this one in one way or another, but let me ask you again to summarize – how do we get attuned with the Godly self on a daily basis? You said yourself that Ego is a part of this dimension and I think I'm giving up the idea of living without Ego totally, but rather pursue the idea of living with Ego peacefully.

SOL: You are right - there is no way you can totally live without Ego. However, there are situations that only time will bring you to where you will automatically *know* that this is not the time to use Ego.

Ego is a psychological defense mechanism and has to do with your choices – these choices are yours and God wants you to use them freely and this is where the Godly attunement comes in. When making a choice, ask yourself what would God say to you and if you do not come up with an answer then let it go and the matter will be resolved on its own. You will find that these matters mostly relate to wanting to control situations, and other people, and making things go the way you want them to go not always with the better good of all in mind. So attunement can be an all-day thing when you are aware that your Ego is in control and you are able to ask yourself if this is the right way to go. Yes, eventually it is all about making a choice and letting go of the result at the same time as making the choice – this is attunement.

CHAPTER FIFTEEN

The Secret of Wavelengths

4 months later

    Zach: Dear SOL, I have many things on my mind today and I really don't know where to start. It happens once in a while that I find myself overwhelmed. It's as if my mind is working overtime and I'm unable to control it.

    SOL: Zach, welcome. As to your thoughts, you are operating on several wavelengths at the same time. Let me explain. In fact, you will notice that I have begun this explanation earlier with Ronny and would like to enlighten you now. This will certainly help bring matters into perspective. It is now time to understand your state of being on this physical dimension. In fact, this is one of the secrets in the Kaballa, which is called the Pardess and that many people can't handle.

Here it is:

You see, you are on a certain wavelength where the universe responds by sending electronic messages, which subsequently control your thoughts. These thoughts arrive as a result of the wavelength you are attuned to. The thing that makes each person different is how you decide to use that thought or whether or not to choose to give it power. This is the secret.

You see, you have been given FREE CHOICE – this is yours to do or not to do. The mind as you know it is actually ONE MIND- all thoughts come from *one* source - THE UNIVERSE – GOD - and they become creation if you as God decide to manifest that. You can do so, or not as you wish. These thoughts come to you depending on which path you are on. You can therefore delete or process- whatever you choose. I am sure you will have further questions on this subject.

Zach: I want to take it slowly as I have a feeling that this is crucial. So let's talk about wavelength which you have mentioned from time to time. I'm not completely sure what this really means so can you please elaborate a little and tell me what wavelengths are? What does it mean to be on a certain wavelength and how can one move from one wavelength to another?

SOL: This physical world in which you live is based on wavelengths. What this means is that an inspiration results from a previous thought which is turned into a feeling - this causes you to be on a certain level of awareness and on this level you are open to certain responses from the Universe. Depending on your level of awareness, you are capable of manifesting certain thoughts which can then be turned into feelings. Your level of awareness will depend on what level of thoughts you are open to from the Universe. In order for a message to be manifested

So when you are on a wavelength – let's say depressed - you allow the Universe to respond to you in kind and what happens is that you become immersed with thoughts from the Universe's think-

Be and it will Be

tank of depressive thoughts, if you will. If your level of awareness is low at the time and you choose to allow these thoughts to enter and manipulate your *mind*, then you will stay in this wavelength or even go lower and become more depressed. But, if you choose *not* to give power to these thoughts and change your wavelength by choosing to delete them and turn your power or wavelength to a higher level then you will find that the Universe will responds in kind. You can then choose to process these new thoughts and thus change the wavelength you are on.

    Zach: So let me see: I am in a certain *state of being* – let's say unhappy - so the Universe will then send me thoughts that reflect unhappiness. If I don't give power to these thoughts –I delete them or let them go– and at the same time choose to think positive thoughts, then the Universe will respond accordingly and this will result in a change of wavelength – from unhappy to happy. This example may sound too simplistic, but I wish to keep it simple so I can understand it better.

    SOL: A funny thing happens when you go on a positive wavelength. The positive thoughts seem to have more power than the negative ones. Imagine that you are in a battlefield - everyone is negative and fighting and shooting each other. Suddenly, *one* person decides to lay down his arms and picks up a white flag. What do you think will most likely happen? Just one person.

Simply, God said when he created you, that you will have everything that you'll need, even your thoughts as they were all pre-created. All you have to do is *choose* - that is all. Imagine that you are in a vacuum which has everything in it you need in order to live, including a bank of thoughts and all you have to do is choose which thought you wish to use. Think of all these as your tools. Just *choose,* that is all. The Universe responds in kind, Zach. So if you are unhappy you will be receiving unhappy thoughts and vice-versa. The physical world however, has a temporal issue, where you may still be responding to old thoughts and actions, in which case it might take a little time and effort to turn things around.

Zach: Let's talk then about how to do this and how long it is likely to take. For example, I have an idea of something I may want to do in the very near future. I believe it will contribute to the good of society and I already have a picture in my mind of how I would like the result of this project to be. Now, this is still on a level of thought and idea and I haven't started doing anything about it. I also have some ideas of what I have to do in order to fulfill this project and I have definitely left plenty of room for new ideas that will probably appear during the process. Now, according to what you say, I have the "right" thoughts, I will do everything in my ability to make them a reality, the Universe will respond accordingly, so this should work, correct? However, you also say that the Universe may still be responding to old thoughts of mine and these could be negative thoughts – but how will I know?

SOL: There are no "right" thoughts, only right choices. It is what you *do* with the thought that counts. So if you are still receiving thoughts, which you do not want to deal with since you are now on a different level of awareness, then simply delete them. I think that what you are referring to are not thoughts but happenings, which have already occurred as a result of past thoughts. In a physical dimension these cannot be denied but you will have to deal with them and at the same time not lose your focus on the new wavelength. Things may take a while longer as a result. As you know there is a saying that sometime you have to go down in order to come up.

Zach: So you have to go down for a while in order to get rid of old negative thoughts and only then can you go up to start anew?

SOL: Absolutely – By God you've got it! Lots of luck and love, SOL.

CHAPTER SIXTEEN

Discover Who You Are

One month later

      Zach: Hi SOL, I'm very pleased that we meet today as I'm feeling stuck and wish to receive your guidance. I can't really explain this, I don't really know what to do and I don't feel very good about myself either. I'm not sure whether I should quit my job, and if so, I don't know what I should do next. I also don't know if I should move an apartment and whether my wife and I should start a family. Whether I should quit smoking again, after I quit two years ago and restarted just recently. All in all, I feel that "stuck" is a good description of me at the moment and the surprising thing is that even a short while ago I felt that I would no longer face these kind of problems. So what do you say about this?

SOL: Well, Zach, How can the Universe help you when you aren't sure about anything yourself? You are confusing the Universe. So first things first - you have to stop being confused. You see, the solution is very simple but on the way to the solution you will bring in guilt feelings, fear, doubt, and probably many other feelings, which will leave you stuck. Want to get unstuck? Follow the rules:

First, ask yourself what it is you do not like about yourself right now. How are you judging yourself? Are you allowing the world to judge you? Are you willing to be in the process of doing completely without doubts and fear and simply trust the process? Once you are in the *state of being,* the life you want will come to you as a result of your *being.* Do not allow the Ego to dictate who you wish to be, but remember when you choose your new *state of being* it should be creative tendencies, which are Egoless and for the better good of all.

I will explain. Say you wish to be a kind person, an honest person. First, feel how that makes you feel and then you will know that it is for the better good of all but it first has to be felt by you

Be and it will Be

– you have to be the experience of it. The Universe will certainly come towards you once you *know who you are* and are not confused. The next step is to simply delete all your negative beliefs. Bringing a child into this world has to happen because two people love each other and want to share that love through another (*love thy neighbor as you would yourself*....) This is not something to be thought about or planned it is something to be felt.

Out of love is the wavelength that will ensure the Universe will respond in kind. The same goes for moving to a new home – *out of love for self and your partner* - for the better good of all is a sure reason for the Universe to respond in kind, and again the same goes for the job. So you see, get to know who you are, who you want to be, and act accordingly.

Zach: There is a tiny little consideration you didn't mention here and that is money! I'm sorry to get back to this again, but my doubts are based on whether I would be able to financially support these changes. I love my wife from the bottom of my heart and I know she loves me, but will I be able to support a newborn child? Will I be able to support a more expensive apartment? And if I quit my job before finding a new source of income, will I be able to support what I have now even before these changes?

SOL: If you read my previous answer you will see that I did take this into consideration. I said that if you act from your heart the Universe will respond in kind. If you remove all doubt, fear, and guilt and out of love *be* in the process of doing, then the Universe will respond in kind. But you have already placed doubt in what I've said by asking these questions. All these questions come out of the very things I mentioned - doubt, fear, and guilt. So what is it? Do you wish to remain stuck or do you wish to get on with it? YOUR CHOICE!

Zach: So let me see, just for clarification. I think I do understand what you say. Let's take the moving-to-a-new-apartment issue as this is something that I am completely sure I want to do out of love to myself and my wife. According to what you say, if this is the reason for the move, I can go ahead and move and then the Universe will respond in kind and provide me with what I need for this move. A more difficult issue is quitting my job before having another source of income. I mean, it takes plenty of courage to do as you suggest and I'm sure that everyone around me will think I'm crazy, not to mention my bank manager.

SOL: I said that first things first. To reiterate, I said, *who are you and who do you want to be?* This precedes everything else because when you *know* who you are and who you want to be, then you will not need to ask all these questions because you will also know *where you are*. You said that at the moment you are confused and do not really respect yourself right now. You have gone back to smoking, for instance. Do you like that about yourself? So how can you say that you are to bring a baby into this world out of love when you do not love yourself? So again, first things first: *know who you are and who you want to be* and then everything else will follow as you will not have guilt, fear, or any other negative emotion that will make you stuck.

Zach: Okay,. One question about this. You spoke of doing things out of love and that this is something that we feel. I can easily relate to this when it comes to my relationship with my wife, but generally I'm more cerebral person and I make most of my decisions on a rational basis and not really through what I feel about the situation. How can I know that my choices are made out of love then?

SOL: The mind governs thought that comes in from the *one mind*, but feelings are a wavelength that comes from within you. When you know love for self you know love for others as self is part of God and God is love. When you are with your wife and you feel good about how she makes you feel you are able to see your self-love, as this is your reflection There is a simple exercise that you can try which will bring clarity into this matter. Remember the *who you are* is not about what is happening outside, it is about your qualities as a person and it would be a good idea to feel how these qualities make you feel. Do these qualities make you feel like a better person? Ask yourself in which way you feel better about yourself – when you preach or when you respect and credit someone by allowing them to be? Is not serenity and humility a better feeling than wanting to control another? Do not get me wrong, I am not saying that you should not pass on knowledge, but that is all that one should do – pass it on and let it go.

Be and it will Be

Zach: Okay, so tell us about this exercise.

SOL: This exercise is a mirror to who you are. As you have learned by now, you cannot recognize a trait in someone else that you do not harbor it within yourself. So in order to discover who you are there is a very simple exercise that will show through others all you have in you and then you can decide if this is who you wish to be, or if you wish to change. What will happen as a result of the exercise is that you will come up against situations that will bring out these traits and you will decide then and there what you wish to do about them. For example, say you have discovered that you have an Ego problem especially when it comes to voicing your opinion and you do not give up until you have had the last word. The exercise will show if you wish to continue or let go of the need to have the last word.

So here goes and good luck:

Take a large piece of paper. Draw a big circle, place a dot in the middle and draw another circle in the middle between the dot and the outer circle. Write down your name in the middle where the dot is. THIS IS YOUR PLAY and you are about to enter all the names of the actors in your play. Begin with the people you are most close to, preferably family or people you grew up with, then extend to anyone else who you feel you have issues with or any type of relationship. If one piece of paper is not enough then use more. Approach this exercise without fear. Remember this is going to lead you to the new you, and your new experiences of self. Remember that all these people arrived in your life because of *who you are*, so if you need to change your circumstances, their attitudes toward you or invite new actors into your new play then you will need to *change* who you are.

    Begin with one person at a time. Say you begin with your father. Write his name on the outer circle. Draw three lines from his name to the middle dot where you are thus forming two columns. In one space write down everything you dislike about that person and in the other space everything you like or love about him. Then go down to the inner circle where you are and turn it all around, write down in one space everything you dislike about that person as if it is you. I.e.: I do not like this or that about myself. In the other space write the good things that you like about yourself, which you liked in that person. Don't argue with this. There may be things that don't fit but leave these well alone and move on to the next one. When you have finished all, you will remain with the inner circle of who you are. You will see clearly that those traits you thought you did not have, which you saw in someone else, will appear in relation to another.

Once you have taken in *who you are*, meditate and bring yourself to a state of awareness, if you are not there already. Ask yourself if you are satisfied with who you are. Hug yourself with your "good" and "bad" traits, or shall I say positive or negative in your eyes. This is very important because you have to accept who you are if you wish to change. This is fundamental. You have to love who you are before you can change or you will stay in the same place because you will not be able to move on and accept all the wonderful humans who brought you these lessons about yourself. How can you accept them if you deny yourself? They are your mirrors, remember?

Once you have gone through this process you will find yourself in situations that will bring you the relevant lessons about self. You will be in a direct state of awareness and then you will know at the very moment it happens what you want to do about it. Choose at all times and you will see how life becomes one big challenge to discover who you want to be. Enjoy!

CHAPTER SEVENTEEN

Surrendering to the God within You

Three weeks later

Zach: Hi, SOL. So I went through the exercise you gave us and personally I had quite a few surprises. I made those long lists about what I like and don't like in other people and turned them around to see, as you said, what I like and don't like about myself – who I am and who I want to be. I had some problems in admitting that I really have some of the traits I found in other people. For example, it was a little difficult for me to admit that I can be quite manipulative, but then, looking deep down, I found that unfortunately I do have this in me, although maybe not in the same proportion that I recognize in other people. Also I found that there can be many contradictions in me. I am generous and miserly, optimistic and pessimistic, rude and kind and so on. I guess that my first question would be if it is one hundred percent accurate that what I see in other people really exists in me. How can I have such contradictions within me?

SOL: Zach, you are human and you are God at the same time. I remind you that creation was set up to discover God in his own image as a human through the senses. All traits are therefore in you as you are not separate – it is just that in each lifetime when you make choices of who you wish to experience, certain traits become more dominant than others and this is your answer as to the proportion. I will say though that there are traits which you will find difficult to accept as yours at this moment, simply because you have not yet experienced those situations yet. But this exercise will certainly help you re-member when you find yourself in these situations.

This whole exercise is the closing of a circle, which began in the beginning of this book when we discussed CREATION + FREE CHOICE = KNOWLEDGE, remember? So this is a technique that will bring you the choice of your creation more quickly and will show you the power within you to be who you wish to be. *The thing is that human*

Be and it will Be

understanding does not grasp that, being who you wish to be, means choosing the human qualities that actually bring you SERENITY because that is when you meet with God. When you meet with the God within you that is when the Universe/God responds in kind. Because you see, when you have God/Serenity you have it all – what else do you need?

Zach: I remember now that you once told me that one of my biggest lessons in this lifetime is to let go of the need I have to be perfect all the times. When I look at the list of who I want to be then I actually see that again this brings me to wanting to be actually a perfect man. I mean, this list consists of really noble qualities such as kind, honest, generous, humble, wealthy etc., exactly what you would expect from a "perfect" human being. On the other hand I remember that such a desire to be perfect all the time is very stressing as it constantly puts me under a very harsh and criticizing magnifying glass. What am I missing here?

SOL: I do not recall "perfect" being on your list. I do remember other qualities which were good human qualities. Believe me, if you mange to be all these qualities you will be serene and humble, and perfect will not enter into this, because the word perfect comes out of Ego – it is the wish to be the best and that is all.

Zach: Well, indeed, perfect wasn't on that list. What I mean though, is what do I do with this now? I know I have those "good" and "bad" qualities in me and I know I want to keep only the good ones, but is it at all possible? Isn't it like wanting to be perfect in a way? And what about the "there is no good and bad" – how does this statement go with lists of good and bad qualities?

SOL: I do not recall having placed the words good and bad in this exercise. What I mentioned are your dislikes and your likes. You see, Zach, we are talking about creating your world. Others may think that what you dislike is a quality they may in fact like and choose that quality. So we are not in judgment here, we are in creation. Who do you, Zach, wish to be? Simple. But you see, you humans have judgments and analyses. I say things very simply but your main "problem", if you like, is that you are non-accepting and disbelieving. But that is the very reason behind this exercise, so that you can actually have the experience of who you are and then know if this sits comfortably with you or if you choose to be someone else. It is all about your choice of what you wish to create for yourself.

Zach: Okay, so what do I do now? I know who I want to be and in fact I also know who I don't want to be. How do I get to the next step, which is *being* who I want to be?

SOL: This is it, Zach, the secret, very simply, *be*. Be in the process every minute, every day. Discipline yourself into your new *state of being*. There is freedom in discipline, remember? It has taken you years of being to *be* who you are. The way to the new you is to *be the new you* as of now and stay being there. It is like an acquired taste. Once you acquire it you will want more. You can choose not to eat rice most of your life and then one day decide to taste it. The next time you taste it, it will be familiar, although not the same. By the third and fourth time you will not understand how you have become unfamiliar with the taste all those years back. You have heard the sentence practice makes perfect? We are not talking about being perfect, we are talking about perfecting your new *state of being*, developing it, creating it.

Zach: What about departing from those traits we don't want to be? I found for example that I do not always trust myself and that sometimes I have a very low self esteem and I have already learnt to recognize when these traits show up and the way they feel and this is what I call when I feel "bad" by the way. So every time these traits show up I experience them and try to let them go. This works sometimes and it does change the way I feel, which I guess shifts me to another *state of being*. But you see, the problem is that these traits keep coming. They belong to specific circumstances that occur from time to time, but I keep finding myself in these places again and again.

SOL: Your will to hang on to these "old" traits is strong and is keeping you from moving on. It is of the Ego. When you come across these traits and you really wish to give them up then all you have to do is *surrender*. God is behind the Ego. He is there all the time and does not go anywhere. You are the only one that moves and each time you allow your Ego to take over you move further away from God. So here it is. Ask yourself, "To what lengths are you willing to go in order to discover a *new* you?" Because I say that in order to discover new "you", you have to surrender the "old ones". You see, your life is linear and by all logic you should be living one day at a time and experiencing one experience at a time. If only you did not have a memory! Well, you do have a memory and you have to find a way of remembering without living your memory. This is where all your problems lie. You really do go forward with time but in your head you actually go backwards. You see, the experience you experienced yesterday is gone but you are still there. I say, say goodbye to yesterday and move forward. It is as if you need permission from me to not feel guilty about enjoying your life and experiencing it. Well, you have my permission because this is all that God ever wanted for you. The saying goodbye is very important and you should realize that the *who* you say goodbye to is part of *who* you are. There are many "whos" inside you as there are many aspects of God. By not departing from the old "you," you cannot allow the new one to enter. Think of it as if there are many characters in your play and that you are only allowing a very few to play their roles. Well, I say that once a character has completed his role in a scene he should be allowed to depart and make room for the next one. This is how you can experience life to the fullest. Everything else is a waste of time. So to recap, understand that the part of you that you do not need any more in order to carry on your journey of self discovery is what this journey is all about. Finding out who you are and who you wish to be, and being that person. I say that this is simple, just *do* it!

Zach: Could you please elaborate on what you say about me not being willing to depart from a negative trait such as feeling guilty with low self esteem. Why are we not willing to depart from something that is not beneficial to us?

SOL: This is where conditioning comes in. This all has to do with patterns you have picked up from your peers. But you are an adult now. The choice is yours. Remember, there is no one in your head except you. You are the buffer or acceptor of the thoughts thrust at you.

I say it again, if you want to move on then you have to depart from whatever is hindering you. Humans have a tendency to hang on to negative thoughts rather than to adopt positive ones, but this is a direct result of conditioning as I have mentioned before. For example, say that you are feeling really good and are having a good day and then suddenly someone tells you some bad news, which has nothing to do with you. Most probably you will insist on feeling guilty for wanting to continue to feel good. And say you do manage to stay feeling good. You will be tested again and again and you will be reminded and perhaps "made to feel guilty by others." That is why I say conditioning, because you do not trust yourself enough to know that you choose how to feel, but you give your power to those who come to you with negative vibes who "make" you feel bad. It is time to reclaim your power and decide for yourself how you wish to feel without being dictated by others.

Zach: I completely agree with every word you say here, but my problem again is in the "how to". How do I depart from these traits I don't wish to experience any more? I mean technically, what do you suggest I do every time I recognize these traits showing up?

SOL: If you see the first sentence of a previous answer you will see that I mentioned your will and *surrender*. So this is how you do it. You surrender *your will* (the Ego) to the God within you. You allow God to take over your life. You do this by first admitting to yourself and to God and to maybe another human being (The twelve steps talk about this) and then you and only you choose to surrender the defect and allow God to take over. You relinquish your control to run the show. You see, this is what is keeping you back; not surrendering your will. You want to be in charge and not let go of your traits or defects.

You see, as you are also God and as God has many, many facets, it is his facets that you wish to adopt as your own. How else can you discover them when you will not let him surface? He is behind the Ego. Allow the Ego to dissipate and God will appear. You can then choose by surrendering.

Let me ask you this: Is God humble? Is he good? Is he serene? Is he honest? Is he generous? Is he loving? Is he kind? Is he beautiful? Is he wealthy? And more? Well, are these not all things you wish in you in order to be who you want to be?

Well, if your answer is yes as I am sure it is, then what would be so bad to *surrender* and allow God to surface rather than your Ego? What I am saying is that in order to just simply *be* the who you wish to be, provided that you wish to be all the good

Be and it will Be

in the world, then all you have to do is *surrender the Ego and move into God* and then you *are*, since God is all the wonderful things you wish for self. There you have it!

All My Love SOL

EPILOGUE

A few days later

Zach: So... I believe we are ready for the epilogue – am I right?

SOL: Ronny and Zach – you have come a great way since we started and this is now the end of this book. There will be another. But that is later on. You have seen that there are reasons and ways to discover who you are and these all lead to learning. You have understood why you are here. You are God in his image and therefore you *are* always. As Zach, as Ronny, you are roles that God plays in your play. You are one and the same.

Life is very precious and it is a commitment to you and your fellow human beings to enjoy the creation of your lives. You have an embedded commitment with God to discover your lives and live them the best way you can for the better good of all. All God ever wants for Himself is for you to be *happy* and to experience life. Never deny this of yourself, whatever you are going through. Be with God, the God in you, in the understanding that all you are doing is creating and discovering who you are. This is what is important, not what you do, but *who you are*. What you do is the result of *who you are*. And if you remember the better good of all at all times, you will always be overwhelmed with satisfaction.

  You see, this is because the better good of all includes *all* of God at the same time. When you do something good for self you are automatically doing something good for all and if you include love - which is God's wavelength - then you have honored God and therefore yourself at the highest level. Remember always to ask yourself if you are acting out of Ego or out of pure love.

  To sum up, this book has led you through a journey of the fundamental question that all human beings come up against which is the key to living well and healthily and with love, and the answer is in this book. It is a message to every human being. If every human being on this earth discovers who they are and thus make the changes to who they want to be, then there will be only peace and solutions and you will all know true Love.

I know that this sounds Utopian, and it is, but you know what? Utopia is feasible and can happen. You simply have to wish it. Begin on your own personal level. That is all you have to do. Have a happy and serene rest of your lives and send this message on to others.

All my love, SOL.

Be and it will Be

ABOUT THE AUTHORS

Ronny Hatchwell:
Ronny Hatchwell, born in Tel Aviv, Israel, but at three months old went to live in Salisbury, Rhodesia with her family until she was ten years old when they left for London, England. Ronny knew from an early age that she was capable of having out of body and telepathic experiences. However, it was not until later in life when, divorced and on the verge of an emotional breakdown, that she received her gift of SOL, channeled to her and changed her life and those around her forever.

Thanks to SOL's teachings, Ronny was transformed from being pessimistic and unmotivated to a life-loving, successful mother and ultimately, CEO of a major music company. Ronny Hatchwell continues to spread the word of SOL through spiritual coaching, providing valuable life-altering tools which she herself has received from SOL.

Zach (Tsachi) Sivan:

At 27, Zach Sivan had many doubts as for his ability to build a successful career. He was also certain it was his genetic makeup which was the cause of his inability to build and sustain a healthy relationship with the opposite sex. But then he met SOL, thanks to Ronny's channeling gift, and everything changed for the better.

SOL has helped Zach, through an amazing journey of self-discovery, to find and sustain a loving relationship with his soul mate and to become the father of two beautiful children. Through his spiritual journey he has also achieved great accomplishments in his career and is now a CEO and partner of a successful software company.